Financial Times Briefings

FT Prentice Hall
FINANCIAL TIMES

In an increasingly competitive world, we believe it's quality of thinking that gives you the edge – an idea that opens new doors, a technique that solves a problem, or an insight that simply makes sense of it all. The more you know, the smarter and faster you can go.

That's why we work with the best minds in business and finance to bring cutting-edge thinking and best learning practice to a global market.

Under a range of leading imprints, including *Financial Times Prentice Hall*, we create world-class print publications and electronic products bringing our readers knowledge, skills and understanding, which can be applied whether studying or at work.

To find out more about Pearson Education publications, or tell us about the books you'd like to find, you can visit us at **www.pearsoned.co.uk**

BRIAN FINCH

Financial Times Briefing on Corporate Governance

**Financial Times
Prentice Hall**
is an imprint of

Harlow, England • London • New York • Boston • San Francisco • Toronto • Sydney • Singapore • Hong Kong
Tokyo • Seoul • Taipei • New Delhi • Cape Town • Madrid • Mexico City • Amsterdam • Munich • Paris • Milan

PEARSON EDUCATION LIMITED

Edinburgh Gate
Harlow CM20 2JE
Tel: +44(0)1279 623623
Fax: +44(0)1279 431059
Website: www.pearsoned.co.uk

First published in Great Britain in 2011

ISBN: 978-0-273-74597-6

British Library Cataloguing-in-Publication Data
A catalogue record for this book is available from the British Library

Library of Congress Cataloging-in-Publication Data
Finch, Brian.
  Financial times briefing on corporate governance / Brian Finch.
      p. cm.
  Includes bibliographical references and index.
  ISBN 978-0-273-74597-6 (pbk. : alk. paper) 1. Corporate governance. I. Financial times (London, England) II. Title. III. Title: Corporate governance.

10 9 8 7 6 5 4 3 2 1
15 14 13 12 11

Typeset in 9.25 Swiss 721 BT by 30
Printed and bound in Great Britain by Ashford Colour Press Ltd, Gosport, Hampshire

FAST ANSWERS TO CRITICAL BUSINESS DECISIONS

As a high-performance leader you need to tackle pressing business issues and deliver hard measurable results. **Financial Times Briefings** give you the targeted advice you need to:

- get to grips with business critical issues quickly
- develop a solutions-focused mindset
- ask the right questions
- take the right actions
- measure the right things
- make the right decisions.

Key features include:

- Clear, concise information
- A focus on actions and objectives rather than theory
- Brief, relevant case studies of success stories and failures
- Benchmarks and metrics to gauge outcomes and achievements
- Briefing lessons to distil key business insights

Financial Times Briefings *series advisors:*

- Jim Champy, author of bestselling business book *Reengineering the Corporation* and Chairman Emeritus, Consulting, Dell Services
- Rob Grimshaw, Managing Director of FT.com
- David MacLeod, co-author of the MacLeod report on employee engagement and non-executive director at MOJ and DfID
- John Mullins, Professor at London Business School
- Sir Eric Peacock, non-executive board member with UKTI and a board member of the Foreign and Commonwealth Office Public Diplomacy Board and Chairman of 'What If' – rated by the FT as the No. 1 company to work for in the UK
- Kai Peters, Dean of Ashridge Business School
- Simon Waldman, Group Product Director at LOVEFiLM

Acknowledgements

I am grateful to a number of people who have generously given me their valuable time to discuss issues of corporate governance. As well as sharing their wisdom and various materials, they sparked ideas and new directions to research. As always, the views expressed in this book are mine as are any errors in understanding. The list includes: Tony Angel, former managing partner of Linklaters LLP; Janice Caplan of Scala Associates; Roger Corley, former managing director, Clerical, Medical; Professors Laura Empson and Bob Garratt from the Cass Business School; Tim Goodman from Hermes Equity Ownership Services; Susannah Haan, secretary general of EuropeanIssuers; Steve Liggins, director of Kencall; Tony Manwaring, chief executive of Tomorrow's Company; Paul Moxey, head of corporate governance and risk management at the Association of Chartered Certified Accountants; Richard Sykes, governance risk and compliance leader at PricewaterhouseCoopers; Martin Taylor; Tim Ward, chief executive of the Quoted Companies Alliance; John Zucker, director of corporate services for Matthew, Arnold and Baldwin LLP.

Contents

[PART ONE]

In brief

The executive précis

Introduction

Corporate governance describes the systems, procedures and behaviours by which an organisation is directed and controlled. Taken literally, it would be limited to companies, as incorporated bodies, but similar considerations apply to a wide range of organisations, from NHS Trusts to charities, quangos and public interest groups.

Interest in corporate governance has grown in response to widely publicised cases where some company directors have run their companies as if they personally owned them, taking unauthorised benefits and unapproved risks, misleading investors, distorting accounts and indulging in insider dealing. The spectacular growth of Polly Peck during the 1980s, followed by its dramatic collapse, built on disquiet aroused by earlier corporate collapses. Cases like these helped create a climate of opinion that something needed to be done to restore investor confidence. In 1991, Sir Adrian Cadbury was asked to look into financial reporting of listed companies. During his committee's deliberations, the Maxwell and BCCI scandals broke, leading to a broadening of its remit and, in 1992, the immensely influential Cadbury Report was published[1].

Good corporate governance should result in decisions being reached properly, with the relevant people being consulted and involved, with conflicts of interest being excluded, with all relevant information considered and with challenging boardroom debate. But it will not stop organisations making mistakes that result in business failure because business and innovation demand risk-taking.

Although public concern has focused on listed companies with public shareholders, good corporate governance principles matter equally to private businesses. It matters to smaller companies when they want to bring in outside investors who require reassurance that attention will be paid to their rights and interests. If the business is eventually sold or listed, then buyers and investors will look at corporate governance for evidence that it is well run so that they are protected against unwelcome surprises emerging later on.

Effects of improved corporate governance

Has an improved climate of governance made any difference? Fraudsters will still find ways to commit their crimes because they will not adhere to codes of behaviour. Nonetheless, they may find it more difficult because of improved controls and because auditors will be more rigorous. Although bullying, discrimination and the excessive power of strong individual personalities will still occur, a change in the climate of opinion within companies and within society has had a beneficial impact.

---

[1] Sir Adrian Cadbury (1992) *Report of the committee on the Financial Aspects of Corporate Governance*, Gee.

What is forcing improvements in governance?

Shareholder activism in listed companies has been encouraged by governments in the belief that information in the hands of shareholders will enable them to hold company management to account. However, the results present a mixed picture. Votes against management remain rare and follow short-term campaigns on immediate issues. Few institutional investors devote resources to long-term struggles with companies they invest in. If they are not happy with a company they often prefer to sell up and invest elsewhere.

Whistleblowing by public-spirited individuals has been encouraged by the UK's Public Interest Disclosure Act, but its successes are also accompanied by disappointments. By 2010, there were 71 cases of NHS Trusts suspending whistleblowers and imposing gagging clauses on them as a condition of a financial settlement.[2] However, despite setbacks things are probably heading in the right direction.

Exhortation through codes of conduct probably does have an impact on behaviours. Codes and accompanying influence from auditors, investors and advisers are directed primarily at listed companies but are beginning to influence private companies.

Regulatory constraint is increasing as a result of the Companies Act 2006, the Bribery Act 2010 and the incorporation of The Corporate Governance Code[3] into the legal framework. The Financial Services Authority is also increasingly using powers to vet directors of companies falling under its remit for satisfaction of a requirement to be 'Fit and Proper' persons.

Debate on corporate governance

The impact of corporate governance is made less effective by severe mission creep. The main areas of creep are into corporate social responsibility and sustainability. Although a consensus has emerged that organisations do owe a corporate social responsibility, what it means and its extent are debated, with no sign yet of a consensus emerging.

A positive outcome of the debate about corporate governance has been a series of shifts in opinion about what constitutes acceptable behaviours. The changed landscape will make it harder for improper behaviour to escape unchallenged. There are more checks and balances in place to restrain and discourage wrongful acts, to improve the way organisations operate and to balance the

---

[2] Nigel Morris (2010) 'Millions spent on doctor 'gagging orders' by NHS, investigation finds', *The Independent*, 2 August.

[3] A voluntary code promulgated by the Financial Reporting Council for companies listed in the UK that fall within the Financial Times Stock Exchange top 350 companies (FTSE350).

interests of different stakeholders. At the margin, those who might have ignored misconduct by others will be less likely to do so.

What is still to be done?

Directors are still appointed as a result of their success in managerial roles with little consideration of the different skills needed at board level. This means that governance at the top is not necessarily translated into good governance (or management) at operational levels. The diversity of British boards is still limited, director development programmes are not widespread and the quality of 'boardroom conversations' remains an unknown. The final big step will be from compliance with the outward forms of good governance to genuine commitment.

What is it? What do I need to know?

2

Introduction

 Corporate governance: describes the systems, procedures and behaviours by which a company is directed and controlled.

The UK Corporate Governance Code describes it as being about 'what the board of a company does'.[1] I think this is much too restrictive because the role of the board is to control and supervise operational management and not just to set strategy and direction. So, if subordinates engage in practices such as price-fixing, bullying or discrimination, the board cannot claim that their governance was good: it was not; these are failings of governance. They reach beyond the boardroom to the implementation of board policies.

Corporate governance is not the same as corporate social responsibility: the latter addresses how the actions of a business may affect the wider or narrower community. Neither is corporate governance synonymous with ethics.

However, what governance covers depends upon a philosophical interpretation of the company and its responsibilities, and these will be strongly influenced by the culture where it is located. For a company located in a country that has a more corporatist approach than the UK, it may be entirely reasonable to hold that governance is as much related to fulfilling a responsibility to the wider society as it is to shareholders. This is an important and complex issue. Demarcations of where corporate responsibility lies are not clear-cut.

As we'll see, it is common ground to most people that a company owes different responsibilities to different stakeholder groups. So, let us say that it owes a responsibility to shareholders to safeguard their investment and to maximise their returns; to employees to ensure their safety and to remunerate them fairly; to customers to supply safe products; to suppliers to behave honestly; to the community not to impair the environment. Individuals within each stakeholder group will hold different views on the balance of these different responsibilities, but there will be a broadly accepted view at any time. For example, the UK Companies Act 2006 codified, for the first time in British law, the duties of company directors. It includes a requirement that decisions should have regard to their impact on the environment. This is clearly to do with a concept of social responsibility and yet it is now undeniably a legal and a governance issue for UK companies. So we will consider these wider issues where they relate to governance, whilst trying to avoid the more subjective value judgements that arise from corporate social responsibility and ethics.

---

[1] Financial Reporting Council (2010) *The UK Corporate Governance Code*, Governance and the code, para 3 (hereafter Corporate Governance Code).

The separation of management and ownership

Corporate governance ideas developed in modern times from the separation of management and ownership in many companies.[2] This is known as the 'agency problem'. It was stated as long ago as 1776 by the economist Adam Smith:

> *The directors of such [joint-stock] companies, however, being the managers rather of other people's money than of their own, it cannot well be expected, that they should watch over it with the same anxious vigilance with which the partners in a private copartnery frequently watch over their own.... Negligence and profusion, therefore, must always prevail, more or less, in the management of the affairs of such a company.*[3]

Where such separation occurs, managers and owners may have conflicting interests. For example, managers may be willing to take much larger risks than shareholders would, in the knowledge that they are not gambling with their own money and can find another job if an uncertain project fails. In other circumstances, they may seek to protect their jobs, at the expense of shareholders, by resisting an attractive offer for the business. However, in the course of a takeover struggle or when there is criticism of poor results, it is often the management who promote a long-term view and investors who err towards cashing in short-term gains. Therefore, governance procedures have developed, initially through the law, to balance these different interests and to protect the interests of shareholders.

However, it is not always clear whose interests should take precedence when different investors have different interests. Banks and bondholders are usually protected through legally binding agreements that provide security, such as debentures. These lenders also have the financial strength to pursue their legal rights.

Shareholders may be in a different position for three reasons:

- different shareholders with different interests
- shareholder inertia
- practical difficulty in enforcing rights.

Different shareholder interests

A company may have formally defined classes of share that have different rights but, even within the same class of share, holders may have different interests.

---

[2] Adolph Berle and G C Means (1931) *The Modern Corporation and Private Property*, Transaction.

[3] *An Enquiry into the Nature and Causes of the Wealth of Nations*, Adam Smith, 1776.

It also raises a potential dilemma for directors: are they the stewards of the interests of the long term traditional shareholders, or the short term activist institutions? Their interests are unlikely to be the same.[4]

Shareholders may include suppliers, customers or even competitors, directors or employees; they may be founding families who still have a significant interest; they may be speculative investors or long-term investors or they may have lent their shares as part of a complex transaction. A competitor who is a shareholder may try to prevent another competitor from taking control of a company, regardless of the attractions of the offer price; or a founding family may have emotional reasons to try to prevent a company being acquired.

 The Korean National Oil Corporation offered £17 per share, later raised to £18, for Dana Petroleum plc in July 2010. Newspapers reported independent shareholders to be keen to accept the offer for the company whose share price had under-performed its sector. However, the Board, led by Tom Cross, who founded the company in 1994, rejected the formal bid that followed as inadequate, although it represented an unusually large 50% premium to the pre-bid price. By late August KNOC reported 48.62% acceptances but still the Dana Board held out. It was reported that Cross wanted £20 per share whilst those independent shareholders were nervous of losing a very good offer.[5] Perhaps Cross wanted to preserve the company's independence more than he wanted a large profit.

Shareholder inertia

Smaller shareholders are particularly powerless. They may be long-term holders who don't follow news about their investments in newspapers and on bulletin boards. They may hold their shares through pension funds, insurance companies or investment trusts who have historically been uninterested in asserting themselves against management and have preferred to sell out rather than get involved in the time-consuming processes of negotiation or litigation. At the end of 2008 around 40% by value of the shares listed on the London Stock Exchange were held by overseas owners, 50% by UK institutions and just 10% directly by UK individuals.[6]

[4] Bob Tricker (2009) *Corporate Governance: Principles, Policies and Practices*, Oxford University Press 218.

[5] Robin Pagnamenta (2010) 'Dana Petroleum chief plots own course', *The Times* 14 August.

[6] Office For National Statistics (2010) *Share Ownership Survey 2008*, 27 January.

Practical difficulties

The law seeks to ensure that shareholders are treated equally, but minority share-holders who are subject to a dominant interest may be unable to afford legal action in defence of their rights. Individual shareholders in listed companies are at a further disadvantage in respect of information. Although insider dealing is outlawed, it is common practice for large companies to meet with and brief their larger institutional shareholders, yet individual investors only have access to equivalent information days or weeks later. In theory, these differential briefings do not cover price-sensitive information but, if they were valueless, then presumably institutional shareholders would not waste time on them.

Further practical difficulties may arise for institutional shareholders, from the complexities of exercising voting rights. The beneficial shareholder may hold shares through a fund manager who, in practice, has the voting rights. Additionally, transactions such as share lending can occur, even without the beneficial owner knowing about it. There are, therefore, businesses that manage proxy voting for companies.

Corporate governance also, therefore, has an important role in balancing the interests of different shareholding groups.

The modern background to corporate governance

The history of corporate governance is one of developing ideas on one side and business scandals on the other, together providing the spark for change.

An important theme of financial scandals is of a dominant individual, often a company founder, who treats public company assets as if they were his own (and it usually is a he).

A second theme is of rapidly growing, entrepreneurial companies running into financial difficulties and resorting to fraud or accounting trickery to deceive investors and financiers in an attempt to keep a struggling business afloat. Although there are instances of straightforward fraud for direct personal gain, these are rare amongst the biggest stories.

Why government takes an interest

Governments have become increasingly concerned about corporate governance of the financial institutions that are critical to modern economies and to that of the UK, in particular (financial services accounts for 25% of UK GDP[7]). So the collapse of Barings Bank in 1995, after one of its traders took enormous bets to try to cover earlier trading losses, was important beyond its immediate consequences. It highlighted a lack of internal control. There were also fears surrounding the

---

[7] Office for National Statistics (2010) *Blue Book*, September, http://www.statistics.gov.uk/downloads/theme_economy/bluebook2010.pdf.

complexity and potential consequences of growing derivatives trading. Together, these brought government attention to trying to limit risks to the economy. This resulted in the Financial Services and Markets Act in 2000, which established the Financial Services Agency. It also influenced government support for reports on governance and for codes of conduct whose remit has extended beyond financial services into the broader business realm.

The financial crisis that started in 2007 showed this effort to have been ineffective and insufficient. While the trigger to the crisis emerged in the US sub-prime mortgage market, the collapse of specific major UK banks resulted from particular misjudgements and poor decisions made in their boardrooms. These failures are bound to have an impact on future legislation and on the development of best practice. They have already led to the 2009 Walker Review of corporate governance in UK banks and other financial industry entities.[8] The crisis has also led to increasing regulation at an EU level (see p. 27).

Figure 2.1 illustrates the forces at work.

We speak of institutional inertia but seldom of institutional momentum. Yet,

Figure 2.1 Drivers of corporate governance

once government bodies start shaping and regulating behaviour, it is hard to stop them. This is because once committees are established and officials appointed to advise them they will not report that nothing should be done.

---

[8] Sir David Walker (2009) *A Review of Corporate Governance in UK Banks and Other Financial Industry Entities*, HM Treasury, 16 July.

The role of business scandals

Most large-scale business failures and scandals have been characterised by weak internal control systems, failure of non-executive directors to exercise control and a dominant chief executive. These have powerfully influenced the growing interest in improving corporate governance. Table 2.1 lists some of the most important scandals.

Table 2.1 Examples of business scandals

1970	Bernie Cornfeld's IOS collapses
1971	Robert Maxwell's Pergamon Press ran into difficulties that resulted in a government inspectors report concluding that Maxwell was not a fit person to head a UK public company
1973	'Tiny' Rowland, chief executive of Lonrho, was subject to a court case to dismiss him, brought by eight of his co-directors on the grounds of his temperament and his concealing financial information from the board
1973	London & County Securities collapsed, exposing managerial incompetence and fraud – perpetrated to falsify published profits and as part of a share support scheme.[9]
1986	Guinness Affair: Following acquisition of Distillers Company, it turned out that the Guinness share price had been manipulated to increase the value of the bid. Several bankers, company directors and wealthy investors served time in prison
1987	Blue Arrow scandal: County NatWest bank executives disguised a failed rights issue and, as investigations continued, other oddities were discovered at Blue Arrow itself, particularly a land deal pushed through by the chief executive: no wrong-doing was proved
1988	Barlow Clowes collapsed in 1988 after it emerged that co-founder Peter Clowes, who was jailed for ten years for his role, had spent more than £100 million of clients' money on private aircraft, cars, homes and a luxury yacht
1991	Polly Peck: Dramatic growth during the 1980s followed by sudden collapse and the founder fled the country to avoid charges
1991	Bank of Credit and Commerce International collapsed, revealing widespread fraud
1992	Robert Maxwell's Mirror Group scandal: Maxwell used the firm's pension fund to buy shares and bolster the company share price

2001	Enron (USA) Liabilities were moved off-balance sheet into special-purpose entities part owned by company executives, creating conflicts of interest, in order to reduce published debt and bolster published profits
2002	Worldcom (USA): Expenses were reclassified as capital to bolster reported profits
2003	Parmalat (Italy) Italian food giant suddenly collapsed. Family businesses had been financed with company money and trading losses had been disguised by accounting fraud
2006	Lehman Brothers (USA) collapse: Using apparently legal accounting devices the bank omitted debt from published balance sheets through repo 105 and repo 108 transactions

Against this background, there was growing international interest in measures to address perceived governance failures. In 1972 the US Securities and Exchange Commission (SEC) called for a standing audit committee of independent directors while, in the same year, the EEC proposed that quoted companies should have two-tier rather than unitary boards – along the German model – and for them to include employee representatives. Then, in the following year, Canada legislated for compulsory audit committees. In the UK, the ICAEW's Accounting Standards Steering Group issued 'The Corporate Report' in 1975,[10] which called for all economic entities to accept accountability to all those affected by their decisions. This was a key step in the development of thinking on corporate social responsibility. It was followed in 1976 by Sir Brandon Rhys-Williams' call for non-executive directors and audit committees which, in turn, led both to a green paper 'The Conduct of Company Directors' in 1977, and to the Bullock Report on Industrial Democracy.[11] This report supported the UK's unitary board system but called for employee directors on those boards.

During the 1980s there was a hiatus but, with a barrage of UK financial scandals at the end of the decade, there was a strong feeling that confidence needed bolstering. This led to the appointment of the Cadbury Committee in 1991, which represents a watershed in corporate governance.

Table 2.2 gives details of UK reports into corporate governance, beginning with the Cadbury Report.

[9] Derek Matthews (2005) London and County Securities: a case study in audit and regulatory failure, http://www.calstatela.edu/faculty/rhayes/524b/Asignments/Other%20Sample%20Cases/LondonAndCountySecuritiesAuditFailureCase.pdf.

[10] Accounting Standards Steering Committee (1975) *The Corporate Report*, ICAEW.

[11] Alan Bullock (1977) *Report of the Commission on Industrial Democracy*, CMND 6706, HMSO.

Table 2.2 UK reports into corporate governance

Report	Reporting date	Commissioned by	Key aspects and main recommendations
Cadbury Report The Financial Aspects of Corporate Governance	December 1992	Financial Reporting Council[12], London Stock Exchange and the accountancy profession	Established the foundations of corporate governance principles in the UK • Voluntary code • Introduced Comply or Explain approach • Supported unitary board • Advocated openness, integrity, accountability • Best practice
Rutteman Report Internal control and financial reporting – guidance for directors of listed companies registered in the UK	1994	The Institute of Chartered Accountants in England and Wales	Report on internal control
Greenbury Report Study group on directors' remuneration	1995	The Confederation of British Industry	Appointed in reaction to 'fat cat' scandals. It focused on directors' remuneration and disclosure of remuneration details. Its main recommendations were: • The appointment of Remuneration Committees • Increased transparency on director's remuneration • Use of external consultants and external comparisons • Appointment of independent non-executive directors
Hampel Report	1998	Financial Reporting Council	Reviewed the success of the Cadbury and Greenbury Reports, consolidated their recommendations and suggested a 'Combined Code' of best practice, which was annexed to the Listing Rules. • Dismissed stakeholder theory • Supported unitary boards • Supported a principles not prescription approach Basically all is well.

Report	Date	Commissioned by	Key points
The Turnbull Report Internal Control: Guidance for Directors on the Combined Code	1999 revised Oct 2005	Financial Reporting Council	Highlighted need for • Review of systems • Report to shareholders • Linked risk management and internal control
Myners Report Institutional Investment in the UK: a review	2001	The Chancellor of the Exchequer Gordon Brown	
Sir Robert Smith Audit Committees: Combined Code Guidance	January 2003	Financial Reporting Council	Instituted in reaction to Enron, detailed the responsibilities of the audit committee and its members
Higgs Report Review of the role and effectiveness of non-executive directors ('NED')	2003	The Secretary of State for Trade and Industry and The Chancellor of the Exchequer Established in reaction to the Enron scandal and to 60% of non-executive directors being appointed without a formal process	Recommended that: • The NED role should be more substantial • Defined independent NED • Should comprise 50% of the board • Should not serve more than six years • The role of CEO and chairman should be separate
Walker Review A review of corporate governance in UK banks and other financial industry entities	2009	The Prime Minister Gordon Brown	Emphasised the required time commitment of chairmen and NED. • Recommended Risk Committee with Chief Risk Officer, taking outside advice, reporting on strategic acquisitions and disposals and reporting to shareholders annually • Recommended Remuneration Committee should be responsible for overarching remuneration principles, be responsible for all high-end employees, consult with risk committee • Recommended that incentive pay should be paid over several years

12 The UK's independent regulator responsible for 'promoting high quality corporate governance and reporting to foster investment'. Its functions are exercised principally by its operating bodies, such as the Accounting Standards Board. Its regulatory powers derive from the companies Act 2006.

The Combined Code of Best Practice was introduced in 1998, revised in 2003 and further revised in 2010, becoming the Corporate Governance Code ('the Code'), promulgated by the Financial Reporting Council and applicable to FTS350 companies. Other important developments at this time were the new UK Companies Act in 2006, the FSA's implementation of the EU's Transparency Directive and, in the USA, the Sarbanes–Oxley Act in 2002 and the Dodd–Frank Act in 2010.

Other international reports and codes that followed the UK's hugely influential Cadbury Report are listed in Table 2.3.

Table 2.3 Examples of international reports into corporate governance

Title	Publication date	Country
Vienot Report	1995	France
King Report	1995	South Africa
Toronto Stock Exchange recommendations	1995	Canada
The Netherlands Report	1997	The Netherlands
Principles of Corporate Governance	1999 and 2004	OECD

International organisations, such as the OECD, have also perceived the economic importance of improved governance:

Good corporate governance should provide proper incentives for the board and management to pursue objectives that are in the interests of the company and its shareholders and should facilitate effective monitoring.[13]

 Shareholder rights

Basic shareholder rights should include the right to[14]:

1 Secure methods of ownership and registration
2 Convey or transfer shares
3 Obtain relevant and material information on the corporation on a timely and regular basis
4 Participate and vote in general shareholder meetings
5 Elect and remove members of the board
6 Share in the profits of the corporation

[13] OECD (2004) *Principles of Corporate Governance*, 2004, 11.
[14] ibid., 18.

The OECD principles have been enormously influential around the world.

This movement on corporate governance has spread worldwide, with codes being developed in countries as distant from each other as China, South Africa and Brazil.

Corporate culture

Corporate culture plays an important part in governance because the informal processes within companies matter as much as the formal ones.

 'Documents recently unsealed in a three-year-old lawsuit against Dell show that the company's employees were actually aware that the computers were likely to break. Still, the employees tried to play down the problem to customers and allowed customers to rely on trouble-prone machines, putting their businesses at risk. Even the firm defending Dell in the lawsuit was affected when Dell balked at fixing 1,000 suspect computers...'[15]

We don't know what specific aspects of company culture may have allowed this to happen but we can say that it could not have happened if Dell had in place just the three outlined below.

 Briefing Lessons

- **Focus on customer benefits not costs.**
- **Work against a culture of fear: admit mistakes early because they get more expensive.**
- **Integrity may have some short-term costs but it has huge long-term benefits.**

Toyota Motor Corporation seems to have had a very similar experience in 2009 with a technical problem leading to runaway acceleration of some of its cars. Denial, accompanied by a lack of swift corrective action, led to humiliation and high cost when the story came to public attention.

Creative accounting

Creative accounting is a major corporate governance issue; first, because it distorts the picture presented to shareholders and financiers and lies at the heart of many business scandals; second, because mild distortion is countenanced by many businesses. It arises because many accounting numbers depend upon

---

[15] Ashley Vance (2010) 'Suit over faulty computers highlights Dell's decline', *New York Times*, 28 June.

subjective judgements. A slightly optimistic view can then become a distortion, but creative accounting takes this judgement a step further. An apparently innocent first step, of putting an optimistic gloss on trading figures, will unwind and need dealing with, which may lead to less innocent distortion to cover it and that, in turn, may eventually require outright fraud to hide the mess. The results are invariably temporary, but reversal over the long term is little help if a distorted picture is given today.

The objectives of creative accounting may be to:

- smooth out profits between accounting periods
- publish improved results now in the belief that trading will improve in the longer term
- meet banking covenants
- improve business valuation to achieve an acquisition or raise new investment
- reduce tax bills.

Good corporate governance patrols the boundaries of creative accounting and prevents decisions that push matters of judgement over the border to the lands of misleading or fraudulence.

Listed companies generally have audit committees but, for smaller companies, this role falls to non-executive directors. The finance director may typically be under pressure from banks and shareholders and therefore also from the CEO. The first governance control should therefore be that the CEO is aware of the consequences of creative accounting; the second is that other directors (including non-executives), aware of their liabilities, ask the right questions; and the final line of defence comprises internal and external auditors.

Individual behaviour

Personal integrity is a key issue of corporate governance that is seldom referred to in studies and reports. The best systems can be subverted by people behaving improperly.

 I worked for a company where, one day, an accounts clerk asked for advice. The company CEO had purchased engines for his boat through the business and, although he had reimbursed it, he had not paid the VAT. She wondered what to do. I was naïve, could not imagine this was deliberate dishonesty and suggested that she had a discreet word with the Company Secretary who could make representations in a way that should avoid embarrassment. She followed my advice, and was promptly fired – which has continued to trouble me for many years and prompted my own decision to leave the company. Clearly the actions had been intended dishonestly and the other directors were complicit. Could systems of governance have helped? The appointment of a senior independent director to field staff complaints might have helped.

Briefing Lesson

- **A pervasive climate of good governance should make it harder for individuals to behave badly.**

The legal structure for governance

The legal structure provides the basic framework for corporate governance. Its core, in the UK, is the Companies Act 2006, which is a consolidation of much previous legislation as well as making some changes to the law. Some things are still governed by UK Common Law, but these tend to be tangential issues. The Act deals with powers, duties and obligations of directors as well as setting out constitutional issues and rights of shareholders. It provides a template for the internal working of companies through model Articles of Association which set out the constitution for a company. This can be amended by shareholders, but it provides the second plank of the legal structure. Beyond this foundation, there is other legislation that affects governance and this is dealt with in more detail under Compliance in Chapter 3.

The basic framework and extended obligations are intended to leave considerable autonomy to organisations to decide their own constitutions and ways of working.

Articles of Association

On top of the legal foundation, the company has two documents particular to it: the Memorandum that sets out its purpose and the Articles of Association that establish its constitution, which must be compatible with the law. The Articles establish various governance issues such as rights attaching to different classes of share, how shares can be transferred and any special conditions, the quorum and notice necessary for different types of meeting (including board meetings), entrenched rights that may require more than 50% of those present to vote in favour, whether the chairman has a casting vote, whether directors are able to vote on matters where they have a conflict of interest, etc. (see also Non-executive directory in Chapter 6).

Other legal documents

Other documents can affect governance. Some private companies have shareholders' agreements requiring the signatories to transfer or vote their shares in certain ways in certain circumstances. In principle, these agreements do not affect the company, since they exist between the shareholders, but in practice they are part of the broader governance picture.

Directors' contracts are also part of this broader picture since they may set out the scope of an individual's work, which can make clear the authority that the individual has to agree contracts, hire and fire staff, etc. They may also detail severance terms, which can be a sensitive element of governance – with considerable shareholder concern arising over large termination payments giving, in some circumstances, a perceived reward for failure.

Current UK developments

At the time of writing at the end of 2010, the UK government has announced a 'comprehensive review of corporate governance practices'. The incoming UK coalition government in 2010 announced a change in policy on company reporting in relation to the OFR (see Communication with shareholders in Chapter 8) introduced and then abandoned by the previous, Labour government, in 2005. 'We will reinstate an Operating and Financial Review to ensure that directors' social and environmental duties have to be covered in company reporting, and investigate further ways of improving corporate accountability and transparency.'[16]

Voluntary codes or legislation?

The relative advantages and disadvantages of regulation and voluntary codes are shown in Tables 2.4 and 2.5, respectively.

There has been and continues to be debate about whether to use legislation and regulation, on the one hand, or voluntary codes, on the other, to improve governance. The British approach has been to have a foundation of law supplemented by self-regulation and voluntary codes, which are based on principles rather than rigid prescription. This has changed over the years, with more leaning towards regulation as Listing Rules and the Takeover Code have gained legal backing but, overall, remains an accurate summary. In addition, the UK has followed a 'comply or explain' regime which means that companies covered by the Code need not follow specific requirements if they believe them inappropriate. However, they are required to disclose the non-compliance and to explain it. The USA, in contrast, has taken an increasingly prescriptive and detailed legal approach, culminating in the Sarbanes–Oxley Act of 2002 which responded to huge corporate scandals.

[16] The Coalition: Our Programme For Government, May 2010, http://www.cabinetoffice. gov.uk/sites/default/files/resources/coalition_programme_for_government.pdf.

Table 2.4 Relative advantages of regulation and voluntary codes

Advantages of statutory regulation	Advantages of voluntary codes
Relative certainty Regulations are generally specified, clearly expressed and outcomes are supported by precedents	**Relatively low cost** It may not be necessary to employ lawyers or other advisers
Enforceability The court system has a system for enforcement	**Speed of judgement** Being outside the legal system, complaints to industry regulators are usually dealt with swiftly
Scale of **penalties** is generally higher **Impartiality** Complaints are not judged by the target's own colleagues or peers	**Flexibility** Through application of judgement to be used to comply with the spirit and allow for practicalities

Table 2.5 Relative disadvantages of regulation and voluntary codes

Disadvantages of statutory regulation	Disadvantages of a voluntary code
Avoidance People may comply with the letter of the law whilst undermining its spirit	**Weak public confidence** May attract accusations of cronyism and failure to control bad behaviour
Legalism Detailed regulation provides a target for unscrupulous people to try to find a way around	**Defiance** Strictures can sometimes be evaded by unscrupulous people
Relatively high cost Detailed rules may impose heavy expenses on companies which need to prove compliance	**Enforceability** Difficult to enforce on companies that trade internationally or that are listed in London but are headquartered abroad
	Box-ticking Apparent compliance, but neither adherence to the spirit nor real commitment to make it work

There has been a proliferation of 'codes' and guidances in the UK that have drawn their inspiration from the Cadbury Report in 1992, including those listed in Table 2.6.

Table 2.6 Examples of UK codes and guidances

Title	Publication date	Promoters/ publishers	Target audience
The Corporate Governance Code	1998, 2004, 2010	The Financial Reporting Council	Primarily directed to listed companies
Good Governance: a code for the voluntary and community sector	2005	The Charity Commission	Voluntary and community organisations
The Good Governance Standard for Public Services	2005	CIPFA[i] and OPM[ii]	Public Service Organisations
Corporate Governance Guidelines for Smaller Quoted Companies	2010	The Quoted Companies Alliance	Smaller listed companies on AIM and PLUS
Corporate Governance Guidance and Principles for Unlisted Companies in the UK	2010	The Quoted Companies Alliance	Unlisted companies
The Stewardship Code	2010	The Financial Reporting Council	Institutional Investors
The NHS Foundation Trust Code of Governance	2010	Independent Regulator of NHS Foundation Trusts	Foundation Trusts
Corporate Governance Guidance and Principles for Unlisted Companies in the UK	2010	Institute of Directors	Unlisted companies

[i] Chartered Institute of Public Finance and Accountancy
[ii] Office for Public Management

The international picture

Although regulation of businesses is largely a matter for national governments, there is a trend towards international regulation, particularly in financial services where entities have significant impact across borders. Prime examples are the The Basel Committee on Banking Supervision, which was originally created by central bank Governors of the Group of Ten nations but now has 28 members, and the EU's Committee of European Banking Supervisors (CEBS). Various inter-governmental bodies, such as the G20, also try to coordinate policies globally. The banking crisis that started in 2007 has had a significant role in accentuating these existing tendencies, resulting in swathes of legislation. The USA, for example, brought in the 2,319-page Dodd–Frank Act in July 2010, accompanied by a presidential claim that it would keep a financial crisis like the one the world just went through 'from ever happening again'.

The same regulating tendencies exist within the EU where a drive towards harmonisation is an additional factor. The EU Commission itself is a body that introduces rules and regulations so, even without the shocks to financial systems, it would tend to do so. This is despite evidence from the USA of heavy costs imposed on companies by the Sarbanes–Oxley Act in 2002, but which still suffered the banking crisis in 2007. In corporate governance, this rush to regulate may prove ineffective whilst having unintended consequences. If compliance becomes box-ticking, then it does not address the behaviours that regulation is aimed at changing; as Tomorrow's Company has reported, 'The current regulatory environment can create a compliance mentality and lead to risk averseness'[17]. Indeed, risk is part and parcel of business and, without it, innovation is stultified.

The European Commission has launched a consultation on whether new laws or guidance are needed at European Union level to improve corporate governance in financial services businesses. The Green Paper floats a series of potential governance reforms, such as new duties for directors, better risk reporting and a wider remit for external auditors. The tone of comments by the EU's Internal Markets Commissioner highlights differences between a UK approach and a more dirigiste culture in some European countries, that may extend to non-financial companies in time.

The ability and willingness of directors to exercise effective control over senior management must be improved: in particular for non-executive directors. Boards of directors too often failed to act as the principal decision-making body of the company or dare challenge decisions and practices. That must change in future. The right balance between independence and skills needs to be struck. I want Directors to dedicate more time to their functions. This can be achieved by limiting the number of directors' memberships in boards. Their expertise must be evaluated more widely, for instance by extending the 'fit and proper test'. I also think more effort needs to be made for a more diverse boardroom.[18]

[17] Tomorrow's Company and The Department for Business, Innovation and Skills (2009) *Tomorrow's Innovation, Risk and Governance*.

[18] Speech by Michel Barnier, 25 October 2010, http://ec.europa.eu/commission_2010-2014/barnier/docs/speeches/20101025/speech_en.pdf.

In 2001, the Commission published a Green Paper on Corporate Social Responsibility,[19] followed in 2007 by a European Parliament report which, amongst other things, invited the Commission to revisit proposals for social and environmental reporting alongside financial reporting; and in late 2010 the Commission launched a consultation on 'Disclosure of Non-Financial Information by Companies'. An EU Green Paper on audit policy (October 2010) posed questions such as whether mandatory rotation of auditors or even some companies having auditors selected and paid by outside bodies might be useful.[20] In late 2010 the Commission is also believed to be looking at issues as diverse as executive compensation, a quota of female directors for listed companies, proxy voting agencies and shareholder identification. Illustrating the points made above, many issues currently the subject of voluntary codes may fall beneath regulation.

Looking further afield, there are two basic requirements for good corporate governance to gain traction in the first place and, thereafter, for voluntary Codes of Conduct to have any hope of working as part of that governance mix. These are:

- the rule of law
- existence of civil society.

There must be a sound canon of law, supported by an uncorrupt judiciary, to provide the necessary foundation of law; and civil society must be strong enough for flouting of rules to carry repercussions. If an individual or company can ignore codes of governance and still have no problem with finding respected professional advisers, obtaining government and NGO contracts and with borrowing money from banks, then the voluntary approach is largely worthless.

The South African 'King III[21] Code of Governance, published in 2009, is widely admired internationally. However, the Sunday Times *reports[22] a study of South Africa's 535 MPs that showed: 7 have been arrested for fraud and 3 served jail sentences, 19 have been accused of bouncing cheques, 71 can't obtain a credit card and 117 have been directly or indirectly involved in at least two businesses that have gone bankrupt.*

The report refers to 'political feelings of entitlement' and a 'culture of impunity'. The paper cites one MP who served only five months of a four-year sentence for fraud in 2003 and has been found to hold six directorships despite being banned from being a company director. He is quoted as saying 'What has the High Court got to do with my life?....I don't have to ask permission from them.'

[19] European Commission (2001) *Promoting a European Framework for Corporate Social Responsibility*, COM (2001) 366 final.

[20] European Commission (2010) *Audit Policy: Lessons from the Crisis*, COM (2010) 561 final.

[21] The Institute of Directors in South Africa (2009) 'King Code of Governance Principles'.

[22] R W Johnson (2010) 'Theft, fraud and violence: South African MP's do it all', *The Sunday Times*, 28 November

Different governance issues take different priority in different countries. In the USA, for example, there remains concern over extreme remuneration packages, executives making it hard to replace the board and instigating 'poison pill' defences to prevent takeover. In Italy and the Far East there are concerns over pyramid-share structures and cross-shareholdings that enable elite shareholders to control large groups through a small minority of the shares. Japan has suffered scandals about gangsters being employed to prevent shareholder participation in meetings.

The USA – The Sarbanes–Oxley Act

In response to the massive company failures of Enron, Tyco, Adelphia Communications and Worldcom, the USA introduced The Sarbanes–Oxley Act ('SOX') in 2002 in order to restore investor confidence. This highly prescriptive legislation has been criticised for high compliance costs that may be damaging to US competitiveness whilst proving ineffective[23] and its approach has not been adopted outside the USA, although UK subsidiaries of US listed companies have to comply as do foreign companies with US listings. Some UK companies, such as International Power plc, which trades in the USA complies voluntarily. Key points of this legislation include:

● A ban on specific non-audit services provided by auditors.
● All non-audit work to be approved by the audit committee.
● A ban on corporate loans to officers, save in the ordinary course of business.
● Established a Public Company Accounting Oversight Board.
● Directors must certify the accuracy of published accounts subject to criminal penalties of up to 20 years' imprisonment.
● Both the company CEO and CFO must certify that '…the report does not contain any misleading or untrue information or any omission of material fact and based upon the officer's knowledge the financial information included in the report fairly represents in all material respects the financial condition and results for the company…' (S 302). They may incur personal liability for mis-statements.
● Management to provide an assessment of their internal controls and the auditors to report on this assessment (applies even to secondary listings in USA) (S 404).

[23] See, for example, 'The Sarbanes–Oxley Act and the making of quack corporate governance', Professor Roberta Romano, *Yale Law Journal* 5 March 2005.

- Code of ethics for senior financial officers (if not why not?) and report any waivers (S 406).

The impact of these controls has been to bolster a compliance industry and mindset that raises companies' costs and diverts executive attention towards compliance.

What is it for?

The purpose of improving corporate governance and what is addressed have evolved over the years since the Cadbury Report in 1992. That was a response to unexpected company failures and major frauds in listed companies and sought to rebuild business and investor confidence. As discussed later, the financial system depends upon investor confidence. If that is replaced by distrust of published accounts and of the behaviour of executive management as stewards of investors' interests, then funding of companies will become harder and more expensive and these problems may threaten the entire financial system.

Legal structures are important in securing confidence and reassuring investors that executive management will be honest and capable, but they are not sufficient. It is impractical for reasons of cost and time for investors and business partners to reach for their lawyers at every turn and to encircle every transaction in detailed contracts and covenants. Fundamentally, business transactions depend upon trust and, without it, the entire system will grind to a halt. As a result, there is a strong public interest in securing and improving corporate governance. This means it is in all our interests, not just because we are customers, suppliers, employees or investors (directly or through insurance and pension schemes) but because it literally underpins the entire economy. But why do organisations and their stakeholders also want it?

Shareholders want:

- Improved board and management effectiveness leading to improved economic performance
- Reduced risks
  - from misfeasance
  - from management pursuing their interests rather than the company's interests
  - from management pursuing poorly considered policies
  - from employees flouting laws and thereby incurring fines or costs in civil actions.

Directors and managers themselves want:

- Protection from overbearing individuals and from each other.

Employees and a host of special interest groups similarly want to protect their own interests or, in the latter case, may have a corporate social responsibility agenda.

So we can see that different groups want different things from corporate governance. In the specific cases listed above, these are not incompatible, but employee interests may become incompatible with the company's economic interests if a factory, for example, becomes uneconomic. The corporate social responsibility objectives of some interest groups may also be incompatible with economic efficiency or other company objectives.

Problems in identifying the purpose of governance are exacerbated when different interests emerge within a class of stakeholder and it becomes clear that these are not homogeneous. This is discussed further below, in relation to shareholders but take an example of employees of a company in financial difficulty that proposes to close a factory.

- Young workers oppose closure because they are fearful for their jobs but are not too hostile because they believe they can find others.
- Older workers are much more hostile because they don't think they will get other jobs.
- However, workers who are close to retirement are in favour of closure because they will receive substantial redundancy payments, leaving them little worse off, and they believe the closure will strengthen the company and protect the pension scheme.

Who is it for?

Use of the term 'corporate governance' has developed to encompass a wider range of ideas and issues. This partly reflects a recognition that many parties, often referred to as stakeholders, have an interest in the good government of the enterprise. These include shareholders, directors, management, employees, customers, suppliers, financiers and the wider community, all of whom have an interest in and influence on corporate governance. Indeed, this idea of a broad community interest in private commercial enterprise is not that modern. Laws governing free trade to control its abuse by monopolists, cartels or profiteers go back at least to Roman times and probably much further. There is a long list of modern UK legislation that controls companies and testifies to the observable fact that the wider community takes an interest in the behaviour of companies. Many reports into corporate governance (see Table 2.2) that have been sponsored by government and prominent business organisations also refer to the interests of stakeholders.

Even at the top of organisations, individual directors need their relationships, powers, obligations and duties defined as do the managers and employees who report to them. Any of them may need protection from exploitation, abuse of power or bullying. Boards of directors are not necessarily homogeneous and an inner circle may form or an individual CEO may exert dominance. Corporate governance provides a means both to express and reconcile differences and to reach balanced decisions. In doing this, it has an important role in making boards of directors more effective and companies more successful.

Customers and suppliers demand to be treated ethically, and the wider community has a developing list of behaviours that it expects from its corporations. These started with prohibitions on monopolistic behaviour but now include fair treatment of employees, employment diversity, minimum pay, environmental concerns, etc.

The organisations covered

The main thrust of the development of corporate governance principles has been towards public listed companies because they:

- are substantial in relation to the economy
- have many shareholders who could be disadvantaged
- have significant separation between management and shareholders and it is practical to address them
- can afford the costs of governance and there are tools available to deal with them.

However, the governance guidelines that apply to these organisations are available to smaller companies too, and those may benefit from observing them, leading to a trickle-down effect of improving standards gradually spreading through the economy.

The reports that have mainly considered large listed companies have also expressed a desire that their principles should be taken up by smaller companies. There is a strong argument that these principles apply to companies of any size. Even though smaller companies are often owner managed or family businesses, conflicts of interest are likely to emerge as they pass through generations and shareholding becomes spread to more distant relatives and to some not involved in the running of the business. For example:

C & J Clark Ltd is a UK shoe manufacturer and retailer based in Street, Somerset. It was started in 1825 by two Quaker brothers and grew to be one of the world's largest shoe manufacturers but, by the late 1980s, it was facing low-cost competition from manufacturers in the Far East, static profits and strongly divergent views about what to do. McKinsey management consultants were brought in and reported in 1988 on ways forward, which included moving manufacture overseas. However, by 1992 the company faced a crisis. Of the shares 70% were split between some 500 family members, many only distantly related to the founding family, with the rest held by employees, trusts and suppliers; they were traded on a matched bargain basis, valuing the business at around £100m. Non-family management had also been brought in more recently, but the four family members on the board disagreed with their policy, called an extraordinary general meeting for October 1992 and tabled a resolution to oust the new chairman, only appointed in May, and another director. Amidst claim and counter-claim from the disputing parties, predators circled. Nonetheless, with views polarised, it was agreed to adjourn the AGM and to explore the option of a sale. In 1993 a £165m offer was tabled by another British company, recommended by the chairman but narrowly rejected by shareholders. The division of opinion is illustrated by the fact that 52.5% of votes cast were against selling the company but this represented 70% of family shareholders. The chairman resigned and was replaced by Roger Pedder, a retail entrepreneur married to a Clark's descendent.

Over the next decade the business was transformed, with much of its manufacturing moved overseas, an increasingly professional approach and a great expansion into overseas markets. In the aftermath of the bitter arguments of 1993 a Family Shareholder's Council was established. It meets regularly with the board and comprises four non-executive and four executive directors: two of the directors are nominated by the Council. A £62m share buy-back in 2002 left 200 family shareholders owning 80% of the company; the balance held by employees, institutions and the Rowntree Trust (a charitable body also founded by Quakers). By 2008 the company reported profits of £111m on turnover of more than £1bn.

 Briefing Lessons

- **Different interests – in this case, it proved possible to buy out those who wanted to sell and to become more family oriented rather than less.**
- **Emotional ties – the case illustrates the importance of non-financial interests.**
- **Vision – the governance of the company is founded on a strong Quaker vision.**
- **Governance – seeks to balance different interests and resolve differences.**

Shareholders may hold shares through an interest in a pension fund which, in turn, holds them through another investment vehicle. And there may be several links in this chain. The attention of those interested in governance began to be directed at the private equity industry because of the realisation of its importance in the economy. In 2006, employment in UK companies controlled by private equity investors reached 1.2m, some 8% of total private sector employment. Total private equity investment in the UK totaled £43bn between 2004 and 2006. Governance guidelines have therefore been developed for private equity investors.[24] Guidelines have also been published for NHS Foundation Trusts,[25] for

[24] Sir David Walker (2007) *Guidelines for Disclosure in Private Equity*, BVCA.
[25] The NHS Foundation Trust Code of Governance, *Monitor,* 10 March 2010

UK charities,[26] for Housing Associations[27] and for public services.[28] Developing interest is not limited to just a few countries; the OECD Principles of Corporate Governance (revised 2004) are immensely influential whilst The International Finance Corporation, part of the World Bank, runs a Global Corporate Governance Forum[29] that is specifically aimed at emerging markets and developing countries.

The community and governance

Nobel prize winning economist Milton Friedman, and others, have argued that a corporation's only purpose is to maximise returns to its shareholders and it is responsible only to them and not to society as a whole.[30] Although they accept that corporations should obey the law, they assert that corporations have no other obligation to society. This is an important view but invites a practical response that society, through government, has always involved itself in private business enterprise, and society is getting more involved in controlling corporate behaviour. Therefore, even if a company's management tries to focus solely on maximising shareholder returns, the scope of laws and the existence of interest groups that apply pressures (that have commercial consequences) means that its focus, in practice, is much wider.

How the wider community affects governance

The community exerts its will in three ways:

- law and regulation
- prestige and economic power
- social pressure.

Law and regulation

Government intervention in the affairs of businesses, addresses:

- what they do
- how they are organised.

[26] The Charity Commission (2010) *Good Governance: A Code for the Voluntary and Community Sector*.

[27] National Housing Federation (2010) *Excellence in Governance: Code for Members and Good Practice Guidance 2010*.

[28] OPM and CIPFA (2005) *The Good Governance Standard for Public Services*.

[29] www.gcgf.org.

[30] Milton Friedman (1970) 'The social responsibility of business is to increase its profits', *New York Times Magazine*.

The UK Factory Act of 1802 was an early example of attempts to protect workers – an example of trying to control what companies do – and, although not very effective, it was the forerunner of many more Acts of Parliament that controlled the behaviour of businesses.

The best example of government direct control of the ways businesses organise themselves is provided by attempts to deal with monopolies.

Standard Oil started as a partnership led by industrialist John D Rockefeller in Ohio, USA, incorporating there in 1870. At the time, oil was used primarily for heating in the form of kerosene. The company grew rapidly, partly by acquisition, achieving economies of scale as well as using aggressive business tactics, some of which were later criticised; for example, it engaged in predatory pricing and struck deals with railway companies that gave it preferential prices based on volumes shipped. These deals made it hard for smaller companies to compete. In its early development, Standard Oil was not one company but many, joined by common shareholdings, and dominated by Rockefeller. In response to state laws that sought to limit the growth of corporations, Standard Oil established itself as a Trust in 1882 that held the shares in its constituent parts.

By 1890 Standard Oil controlled 88% of the refined oil flows in the USA and, in that year, Congress passed the Sherman Anti-Trust Act that 'forbade every contract, deal, scheme or conspiracy to restrain trade'. In 1892 the state of Ohio compelled Standard Oil of Ohio to be spun off as a separate company, but it was still controlled by the main company. By 1904 Standard controlled 91% of production and in 1909 the US Justice Department brought proceedings under the federal antitrust law that eventually resulted in its break-up into 34 companies.

This tradition of legal intervention has expanded to cover a wide range of matters: from minimum wages, to terms and conditions of employment, health and safety, staff redundancy, diversity and discrimination, the environment and animal rights, etc. In addition, the very constitution of companies is set within a legal framework.

Prestige and economic power

As the state has grown to comprise a large share of modern economies, governments often impose their will through their prestige, buying power or even threats.

In 2010 an oil well being drilled in the Gulf of Mexico under the ultimate control of BP suffered a blowout which resulted in 11 deaths and a massive oil spill that threatened the environment and the economic interests of millions. US public opinion was strongly critical of the company, but the role of president Obama and the US legislature was noteworthy. The administration, the president himself and many legislators inveighed against BP. Whatever the reasons and causes behind this, it inflicted an enormous extra-judicial punishment on the company and exerted pressure to agree a huge compensation fund outside the normal legal processes.

This powerful example of the state exerting influence in extra-legal ways also illustrates the effect of politics in such processes. At the same time that US politicians were attacking BP, the US government was resisting attempts by India to seek compensation from a US company for the Bhopal environmental catastrophe in 1984 that resulted in at least 2,000 deaths and tens of thousands of long-term injuries. Leaked emails in 2010 showed Michael Froman, US Deputy National Security Advisor, responding to India's request for support in obtaining World Bank loans by raising concerns about an apparently unconnected issue – the attention being directed to Dow Jones, successor company to Union Carbide that owned the plant where the accident occurred.[31]

Social pressure

Finally, society exercises its will through pressure in two non-legal ways:

- the climate of opinion – that gradually influences individual behaviour
- the importance of reputation to most companies.

Climate of opinion

The climate of opinion manifests itself in complex ways.

- Formal influence, perhaps through membership of professional bodies that are subject to disciplinary codes or the stock exchange listing requirements that apply to public companies or accounting standards that apply to all companies.
- Single issue activists such as environmentalists, animal rights groups or anti-apartheid campaigners influence the climate of opinion in ways that can lead eventually to economic pressure through consumer boycotts or to political pressure through the influence they have on governments (e.g. Nestlé and others responding to Palm Oil campaigners).[32]
- Informal social structures and journalism are important. Seeing persistent criticism in the press and knowing that friends, relatives and colleagues are reading the same things must influence directors and employees of companies.

Company reputation

Reputation matters because a company's customers, suppliers, employees, financiers and shareholders are members of society; as are legislators and

---

[31] James Lamont (2010) 'Obama accused of muting Bhopal disaster', *The Financial Times*, 20 August.

[32] 'The other oil spill', *The Economist*, 24 June 2010.

regulators. So there are many direct and indirect sanctions that can communicate the unpopularity of a policy or course of behaviour as well as approval. Sales, employee motivation and recruitment can all be affected by favourable or adverse publicity and may have an impact on company profits.

This brings us back to important distinctions: corporate governance is not corporate social responsibility ('CSR'), nor is it ethics. However, there are important relationships between these three things. Governance is a set of systems, procedures, practices and behaviours that control how the company organises itself to do things; CSR comprises things the community thinks the company should (or should not) do, that have an impact on the wider community; and ethics describes community norms of how individuals and companies should behave. So there may be a community consensus on a diverse range of matters, such as charitable giving, environmental protection, employment conditions of suppliers. This is social responsibility, not governance. However, having made the distinction, we can see that it is difficult to unravel their interconnectedness. It is the behaviour of companies that upsets their shareholders or society rather than exactly how it was decided to do those things.

Size and structure of company

The scope of corporate governance processes must be appropriate to the size and structure of the organisation, which has been recognised in the reports listed in this book. Commercial organisations may be:

- owner managed
- private
- public
- listed small or large.

At the owner-managed stage, governance is most likely to focus on communication with employees, customers and financiers and on compliance with legal requirements. As outside shareholders become involved, they seek the introduction of processes to ensure they are informed and their interests protected. The founder may also take on outside directors for their advice and perspective. As ownership is transmitted to the next generation, a system incorporating an informal family council may emerge to balance the interests of family members involved in the business with those who are not. An important stage occurs as non-family or non-shareholding executives become important in a business and more formal governance procedures may be introduced for a variety of reasons, ranging from balancing management with ownership interests to reassuring outside stakeholders. And these changes are not just related to size; while governance requirements are imposed on public companies and more stringent requirements on larger ones, substantial private companies often voluntarily adopt sophisticated governance processes.

The objectives of good corporate governance

As the purposes of good governance have shifted, so have the levers it uses. Today these are primarily:

- transparency
- control conflicts of interest
- balance stakeholder's interests
- equality of information
- reduce risks
- effective management.

The first four of these relate specifically to balancing the interests of different stakeholders. Transparency should give shareholders full, timely and accurate information on which to base considered opinions. Conflicts of interest between shareholders and management and other stakeholder groups should be controlled through governance procedures and, in this context, it is important to ensure that all stakeholders get the same information at the same time. Then we move on to reducing the risks arising from the sort of issues listed above and end, finally, with the objective of more effective management.

Internal efficiency

Agency theory is the dominant theory of how companies operate, but 'board dynamics' may be equally important.

- Is there an inner board?
- Is there a dominant individual or group?
- Are board members cooperative or combative?
- Is the board well managed?
- Is the top team focused?
- Relationships between the board and top management?

The board knows only what it is told, although its members can ask probing questions. Therefore, the top team may control the board through information denied or slanted.

Why do it? Risks/rewards

3

Introduction

There are four broad reasons for companies to institute good corporate governance procedures:

- compliance with the law and regulations
- stakeholder demands
- improve corporate effectiveness
- public and employee relations benefits.

Compliance

The first of these recognises considerable swathes of corporate governance, corporate social responsibility and ethical behaviour ordained by law, beginning with The Companies Act 2006. In addition, for listed companies, there are listing requirements imposed by the stock exchanges and backed by the Financial Services and Markets Act (2000) that add further obligations, particularly surrounding reporting but also relating to their internal governance.

There are two types of such law. The first type applies to particular industries, such as The Financial Services Act applying to investment companies and the Gaming Act (1968) to gaming companies. The second type has general application but adds particular obligations on directors and on companies that effectively comprise governance issues.

Insolvency Act (1986)

Whereas directors owe their duty to their company, this changes to a duty to protect creditors' assets at the point where 'there is no reasonable prospect that the company would avoid going into insolvent liquidation'.[1] Exactly when this tipping point occurs may be hard to define precisely, particularly when the directors are hoping to secure an order or significant funding or to reach an informal agreement with creditors that will secure the future of the company. In such circumstances, expert advice may be needed, but actions that are being taken should be well documented, whether by board minutes or notes of meetings and telephone conversations.

Bribery Act 2010

Bribery and corruption are serious problems when trading in many countries. Whilst the UK is generally viewed as a business environment where bribery is rare, it would be a mistake to imagine it is entirely absent.

[1] Insolvency Act 1986 S214(2) and The Companies Act 2006 S172(3).

Bribery increases business costs and encourages further, unpredictable demands. It also has potential to eat away at the internal probity of the organisation that gives bribes.

 Abco is a medium-sized business established in an African country that also trades in neighbouring countries. In one of these, there was an unexpected tax demand from the authorities that had to be paid up-front before an appeal could be lodged to recover it. The money was duly paid and the appeal was lodged and, after many meetings, it was agreed that the money would be repaid. Nothing happened. More meetings, telephone calls, letters. Nothing happened. Finally, at a meeting in a hotel coffee shop, an official blatantly and openly demanded a 'bribe'.

The directors decided not to pay but to continue trying to recover the money through official channels. Although there was little risk of being caught giving a bribe, that was still a consideration; there was also an ethical argument. But, above all, what message would it give to the company's own accounting staff?

 Briefing Lesson

- **The person who gives a bribe is also corrupted, having taken a first step away from moral probity. What may be the second step? What example and message does it communicate to other employees in a position of trust who become aware of it?**

The US Foreign Corrupt Practices Act (1977) makes it a crime to bribe a foreign official overseas.

 In December 2010 The Times *reported a US application to extradite a solicitor from the UK who is alleged to have acted as middleman for a US company to bribe executives of a Nigerian company. The alleged crime did not occur in the USA and the solicitor is not a US citizen.[2]*

 Briefing Lesson

- **Bribery is not just illegal in the country where it takes place but often in the country where the giver of bribes lives or their business is established.**

---

[2] Alex Spence (2010) 'Solicitor facing bribery charges urges court to halt extradition', *The Times,* 2 December.

The UK's Bribery Act (2010) goes further, creating:

- two general offences covering the offering, promising or giving of an advantage, and requesting, agreeing to receive or accepting of an advantage
- a discrete offence of bribery of a foreign public official.

The Act also creates a new offence of:

- failure by a commercial organisation to prevent a bribe being paid for or on its behalf (it will be a defence if the organisation has adequate procedures in place to prevent bribery).

 The penalties may be severe – a fine and/or up to ten years' imprisonment for an individual.

The last point creates a new need for companies to have adequate procedures and to document and police them adequately. This requires clearly expressed ethical standards, staff training, careful auditing of payments to identify what they are for and close monitoring of expense claims. The legislation refers to gifts and provision of hospitality as possibly unlawful activity. The liability has also been potentially extended to actions of contractors or agents of the company, which requires due diligence on supply chains, special clauses in supply contracts and careful monitoring of the reasons for and destination of payments.

For all these offences the company faces an unlimited fine. To illustrate the likely scale of these, Mabey & Johnson, a UK company, reported concerns about its past actions to the Serious Fraud Office, which resulted, in July 2009, in fines totalling £6.6m.[3]

The Department of Justice has produced draft guidance notes[4] on adequate procedures to prevent bribery, which specify six principles:

1 Proportionate Procedures
2 Top-level commitment
3 Risk Assessment
4 Due diligence (on business partners)
5 Communication
6 Monitoring and review.

[3] Serious Fraud Office (2009) 'Mabey and Johnson Ltd sentencing', Press release, 25 September, http:// www.sfo.gov.uk/press-room/latest-press-releases/press-releases-2009/mabey--johnson-ltd-sentencing-.aspx.

[4] Ministry of Justice (2010) *The Bribery Act 2010 Guidance*, http://www.justice.gov.uk/guidance/docs/bribery-act-2010-guidance.pdf.

The introduction emphasises government expectation of courts applying common sense in interpreting the law, which should not lead to burdensome procedures. It reiterates that facilitation payments are generally unlawful, but indicates that companies listed in London but not trading in the UK may not be covered. It also highlights proportionality, both in connection with what entertainment expense may be reasonable and in what procedures are appropriate to the size and scope of the company and risks of bribery it faces. This is also an enveloping first principle of putting appropriate procedures in place (albeit they need only be proportionate to the circumstances); that leads on to top-level commitment to observe the legislation, which informs analysis of risks arising from aspects such as the country where business takes place, the industry, size of contract and people involved. This leads on to a principle of conducting due diligence on business partners, local customs and relationships. The fifth principle of communication demands that companies communicate their commitment to the legislation and also the detail of their preventative procedures to internal staff and to business partners. The final principle is to monitor and review the effectiveness of procedures through mechanisms such as financial control systems, staff questionnaires and external verification.

The final quarter of the guidance is not formally part of it, comprising illustrative case studies, which raises the question of what view the courts will take when cases come before them. It is unknown what weight they will give the guidance nor how much common sense will be applied.

Health and Safety at Work etc. Act (1974)

A director, as well as the company, can be liable as an employee under Sections 7 and 8 or as a result of consent, connivance or neglect, so that:

> (1) Where an offence under any of the relevant statutory provisions committed by a body corporate is proved to have been committed with the consent or connivance of, or to have been attributable to any neglect on the part of, any director, manager, secretary or other similar officer of the body corporate or a person who was purporting to act in any such capacity, he as well as the body corporate shall be guilty of that offence and shall be liable to be proceeded against and punished accordingly.
>
> (2) Where the affairs of a body corporate are managed by its members, the preceding subsection shall apply in relation to the acts and defaults of a member in connection with his functions of management as if he were a director of the body corporate.[5]

---

[5] Health and Safety at Work etc. Act 1974, S37.

Under the Company Directors Disqualification Act 1986, the penalty may be a fine and/or up to two years' imprisonment or disqualification on conviction under indictment. A handful of directors have been disqualified. A maximum of 15 years is available for the most serious offences such as those where they have been disqualified before.

In an extreme case a company can be prosecuted under the Corporate Manslaughter and Corporate Homicide Act 2007, which provides for unlimited fines as well as whatever remedial order the court may think fit.

Beyond this legal foundation, there are other regulations that may also affect governance procedures. These include the Listing Rules, which also give legal force to the Code and the Takeover Code, for companies whose shares are quoted on public exchanges and also the Disclosure and Transparency Rules. There are also accounting standards that affect companies' internal procedures; so an obligation to consider business risks or to certify that a business is a going concern implies certain processes to be followed by company boards.

Stakeholder demands

The different stakeholders in a business each, in their way, apply pressure to improve corporate governance. Shareholders and employees, for example, both seek greater transparency and better information flows. Points of conflict between stakeholder interests can lead to adverse publicity or other consequences. For example, shareholders who have lesser voting rights may seek their equalisation as part of the price of new equity; environmental groups may campaign for greener policies; unions may campaign for improved rights for foreign workers.

Corporate effectiveness

Whereas the first two points relate to outside pressures, improved management effectiveness is frequently desired by the management itself. For example, the board at war with itself is seldom effective. Vital information is withheld from colleagues, decision-taking may be slow and decisions may be sub-optimal, time is wasted on internal feuds rather than essential tasks, subordinates become disenchanted and demoralised. Another example is that the board dominated by a powerful individual and that does not take account of dissenting opinions often ends up making bad decisions. The way the board operates and the company organises itself can therefore be critical to performance.

The original purpose of non-executive directors was not to assist with corporate governance but to provide an outside view, independent advice, wisdom and specialist skills in order to assist the board to reach better decisions. This goal of improved effectiveness remains a major reason for recruiting non-executive directors.

Public and employee relations

The fourth motivation for corporate governance is that it benefits the company and its performance. A company that is seen to be well governed and to be sensitive to corporate social responsibility issues will benefit from an improved image that will enhance:

- staff recruitment and motivation
- employee behaviour
- brand image and customer relations.

Recruitment and motivation

The company that is admired will be an attractive place to work and will find it easier to recruit high-quality individuals. That employers believe this to be true is evidenced by the keen competition to feature on the Times – Best Companies to Work For lists. Once recruited, there is evidence to support a high correlation between employee satisfaction and company performance.[6] Whilst it is hard to prove that directors who are believed to overpay themselves damage the morale and motivation of their subordinates, it seems likely that this is the case.

Employee behaviour

Although employee behaviour may seem to be the same issue as motivation, there is an important difference that is worth noting. It is that bad behaviour by directors or senior executives may find itself mirrored by their subordinates. Thus a company that pays bribes to secure contracts may find employees feel that dishonesty is countenanced. Similarly, behaviours such as bullying are likely to cascade through an organisation.

Brand image and customer relations

It is clear that the image of a brand is important both to many consumer product manufacturers and also to industrial companies. They recognise that in wearing a label customers buy the image as much as the product. That is why designer products have a market despite carrying a premium price.

The costs of good governance

There are undoubted costs of good governance because the demands for checks and balances, for constraints and for extra reporting all have a financial cost. However, the most important of these are hidden costs resulting from the

[6] Janice Caplan (2010) *The Value of Talent*, Kogan Page.

diversion of senior executive time to comply with governance requirements. These costs can, of course, be mitigated for smaller companies. Unlisted companies may follow best practice but adjust their compliance to ensure that the burden of cost is proportionate; and the Code itself makes suggestions for mitigation, such as two non-executives on a nomination committee rather than three or more for a larger company.

Disclosure and reporting requirements are mostly contained in legislation and are unavoidable. The most significant financial costs relating to compliance with the Code are probably those relating to non-executive directors:

- NED appointments required to be 50% of board
- extra costs of induction, briefing and training
- higher payment
  - to ensure they are able to devote sufficient time and commitment to meet expanding governance demands
  - to sit on board committees
  - for external advice such as on remuneration and audit.

Other matters, such as regular board evaluation and using outside facilitators for this, will add to costs, as will requirements to search widely for non-executive directors rather than appointing friends and acquaintances and not appointing a new chairman from within the company. However, all these measures should make directors and boards more effective.

There are also constraints imposed by good governance that may not strictly impose cost but will change the way a company operates. An example might be the recommendation of the Code not to reappoint non-executive directors to serve for more than nine years.

The risks of corporate governance

There are limited extra risks imposed on organisations from following good governance procedures. The most significant is probably slowing effective, entrepreneurial decision-making through the need to consult the full board, unless a particular decision has been formally delegated by it. On the other hand, such risks are generally more theoretical than real. If a decision is so urgent that it must be made without there being time to prepare briefing documents and analysis for distribution, then it is probably unwise to take it. If the decision entails a relatively small commitment, then a director or senior manager is probably empowered to take it without referral; if not, then a telephone conversation should be sufficient to get authorisation; if even that is not possible but the commitment is small and the advantages manifest, then an executive would probably take the decision and seek authorisation afterwards. If none of this is possible, then the commitment is probably substantial and those are just the circumstances that justify an insistence on proper board review.

Even the possible adverse effects can be mitigated by adjusting compliance with best practice to the size of the company, such that the burden is not disproportionate to the risk. Most of the codes of conduct and even some requirements of the Companies Act adjust their requirements by company size and by whether the company is quoted or not.

The requirements of transparency may risk revealing strategies to competitors as well as to investors. But, again, good governance in the UK is on a 'comply or explain' basis so that directors can withhold information and explain its sensitivity.

In very limited circumstances there may be the risk of constraining a company's ability to recruit key people. Insistence on a wide search and making appointments through a nominations committee could conceivably stand in the way of selecting someone who has a perceived conflict of interest. An example would be the case described below where James Murdoch was appointed as chief executive of BSkyB. Another would be the appointment in November 2010, to head the UK subsidiaries of Banco Santander, of Ana Botin, whose father heads the Spanish parent and whose grandfather founded the bank. However, in both these instances the appointee has excellent credentials for the post.

The rewards of corporate governance

There are three broad categories of benefit to be expected from improved corporate governance:

- improved organisational effectiveness
- risk reduction
- balancing stakeholder interests.

Organisational effectiveness

One of the objectives of good corporate governance is a more effective board and a more effective organisation. Without effective constraint, for example, an over-mighty CEO or chairman may damage a company through pursuing egotistical projects and self-gratification. The better argument for improved effectiveness is that accepted principles of governance aim to add a wide range of relevant experience to boards so that they do not just constrain but also add wisdom to decision-making. However, there is only weak evidence of higher returns to shareholders from companies with better corporate governance and, what there is, seems to relate to management protection and unfairness such as:

- poison pill defences against takeover
- unequal share voting rights.

Risk reduction

Good governance aims also to establish systems and procedures that reduce or prevent fraud, misallocation of resources and unlawful behaviour. The reward of such prevention is the saving of potential fines and damage to the company's reputation.

We discuss elsewhere whether governance works, but what are the risks of failure? Well-price fixing has to be an example of corporate governance failure and examples of its costs include:

- Fines totalling £248m levied on 9 DRAM chipmakers in 2010 by the European Commission.

 Nine chip makers have been fined 331m euros (£283.1m, $404.2m) by European Union regulators for illegally fixing prices of DRAM chips. The companies included household names such as Samsung, NEC, Hitachi, Mitsubishi and Toshiba. A 10th chip maker, Micron, escaped a fine in return for alerting the competition authorities.

The cartel, in operation between 1998 and 2002, involved a 'network of contacts' who shared secret information. They colluded to set prices for DRAM chips sold to major PC makers and server manufacturers, the commission said. The penalties mark the first settlement decision in a cartel case in which companies received a 10% cut in penalties in return for admitting involvement.[7]

- In 2003 enquiries in the UK in relation to price-fixing on football shirts involved JJB Sports, Allsports, Umbro and the Football Association, with fines totalling £17m.[8]
- A dozen tobacco manufacturers and retailers, from supermarkets to petrol station operators, have been fined a record £225m by the Office of Fair Trading (OFT) for unlawfully inflating the cost of cigarettes.[9]
- Several of Europe's leading vehicle makers are under investigation by the OFT for price-fixing.[10]

[7] 'Chipmakers fined by EU for price fixing', *BBC News*, 19 May 2010.

[8] Devika Bhat (2007) 'JJB sport faces legal action over price-fixing', *The Times*, 8 February.

[9] Richard Wray (2010) 'OFT levies £225m fine for cigarette price fixing', *Financial Times*, 15 September.

[10] Michael Peel, John Reed, amd Michael Schaefer (2010) 'OFT targets truckmakers', *Financial Times,* 15 September.

There are personal costs as well as business ones. Bribery is another failure of governance:

> ...the former chief executive of PWS, a London based insurance broker... was prosecuted by the fraud office after the case was referred by the Foreign and Commonwealth Office in October 2005. He was accused of presiding over a network of corrupt payments during his time as head of the company's American division before he became chief executive.' He oversaw 41 illicit payments to senior officials at Instituto Nacional de Seguros (INS), the Cost a Rican state insurance company....[11]

He was jailed for 21 months.

Good corporate governance does not insure the company against making bad decisions.

> *In 2010 The UK's Prudential Insurance, a company with a stock market valuation of around £5bn, made a £22bn offer for AIA, the Asian arm of the giant US insurer AIG that failed in the wake of the financial crisis of 2007. This would have involved a £14bn rights issue, possibly a sale of the original UK business and a complete reorientation of the company. There was an unusual degree of opposition from institutional Prudential shareholders. Whilst recognising that Far Eastern markets were growing rapidly, they felt the price being offered was too high in the context of the high risks associated with such a fundamental change in the business.*

Balancing stakeholder interests

The economic rewards of balancing stakeholder interests are self-evident in so far as this is a zero-sum game. For example, where a management team flouts good governance and over-rewards itself, it transfers value from shareholders – £1 gained by them is a £1 loss to this other class of stakeholder. Similarly, protecting the organisation against conflicts of interest prevents unfair enrichment at the expense of others.

But things are not always so clear-cut and the different interests of different stakeholders may not always be in total opposition:

> *Australian media tycoon Rupert Murdoch's News Corporation owns UK newspapers such as The Times, News of the World and the Sun, accounting for some 30% of the country's print news media. In the late 1980s, with the liberalisation of broadcasting regulations and the development of plans for pay TV in Europe, he invested heavily in the new*

---

[11] Alex Spence (2010) 'Insurance chief jailed over $2m bribes to win foreign contracts', *The Times*, 26 October.

technology. In 1990, with heavy costs and risks threatening the two UK players in this market, he merged his Sky Television with its rival, British Satellite Broadcasting, giving his News Corporation 50% of the merged entity and the right to appoint five directors to the board and to hold the chairmanship. In effect, it was a takeover by Sky, with most of the top jobs going to its employees.[12] The business was floated in 1995, reducing News Corporation's stake to 35% but not its apparent influence, with the Guardian writing that Murdoch 'is perceived as exercising absolute control.[13]

Eight years later, in September 2003, newspapers reported, 'City fund managers lined up to express dismay at Mr Murdoch's apparent move to install his son, James, as the satellite broadcaster's new chief executive'.[14] He appeared well qualified, having proven very successful in managing News Corporation's Star TV business in the Far East; however, a fund manager was quoted as saying, 'People are simply worried about a family appointment at BSkyB'[15] and the same report continued 'One big institution said it would be asking for specific information about the process….to find a successor for [the present chief executive].'

Previous governance concerns, apart from Murdoch's dominance from a minority shareholding, included the lack of a nomination committee and the lack of clear performance criteria for share awards.[16] There were also issues about the independence of supposedly independent non-executive directors. Despite tough talk to journalists (my emphasis added),

'Some of BSkyB's biggest shareholders yesterday delivered an **ultimatum** *to the satellite broadcaster, telling senior non-executive directors they will not accept a simple shoo-in of James Murdoch…' and ' the 10 institutional shareholders* **summoned** *Royal Mail chairman Allan Leighton and former leader of the House of Commons, Lord St John of Fawsley – both independent non-executive directors of the company – to an emergency meeting…' and '…the selection process must be rigorous and objective'.[17]*

the boss's son was duly appointed.

Was Murdoch snr chastened by the outcry? Not a bit. A year later another outcry resulted as BSkyB introduced a share buy-back scheme that led to News Corporation increasing its percentage stake, first to 37% and then to 39%. Investors were mollified by a 26% increase in operating profit. Then, to prevent the possible emergence of a significant competitor, in 2006, BSkyB bought 17% of 'free to air' broadcaster ITV, to block its acquisition by cable company NTL, again to a public outcry.

[12] 'Sky executives in control at BskyB', *Media Week*, 30 November 1990

[13] Dan Milmo and Gill Treanor (2003) 'BskyB and City clash over succession', *The Guardian*, 17 September.

[14] ibid.

[15] ibid.

[16] ibid.

[17] Jill Treanor and Dan Milmo (2003) 'BskyB investors reject a Murdoch "shoo-in"', *The Guardian*, 24 September.

Briefing Lessons

Does this tale show that a determined tycoon can flout governance strictures? I think that is the wrong interpretation and the relevant points are different.

- 'Hilary Cook, the director of investment strategy at Barclays Private Clients, said: 'When you buy the shares, you have to accept the way Rupert Murdoch runs his companies. He walks sideways around rules...Sky has been an extraordinary success story'.[18]
- Shareholders are far more interested in performance than in governance: it is failure that prompts them to act decisively.
- Non-executive directors generally take the same viewpoint: it is performance that matters.
- These episodes actually illustrate significant change in attitudes to governance. They can be seen as a series of warning shots. When economic interest is at stake, investor groups and independent non-executive directors may prove much tougher.

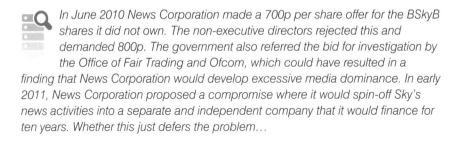 *In June 2010 News Corporation made a 700p per share offer for the BSkyB shares it did not own. The non-executive directors rejected this and demanded 800p. The government also referred the bid for investigation by the Office of Fair Trading and Ofcom, which could have resulted in a finding that News Corporation would develop excessive media dominance. In early 2011, News Corporation proposed a compromise where it would spin-off Sky's news activities into a separate and independent company that it would finance for ten years. Whether this just defers the problem...*

 Briefing Lesson

- It is underlying interests that determine actions and good governance is a tool to protect those interests: it must not be seen as an end in itself.

---

[18] Saeed Shah (2003) 'Appointment of James Murdoch at Sky sparks succession debate', *The Independent*, 15 February.

Does good governance work?

The evidence that improved governance leads to improved performance is mixed. This is partly because of the entanglement of cause and effect; perhaps high performing companies are those most likely to devote resources to governance issues. There are also different aspects of governance and proving improved performance may depend upon which ones are measured. It is possible, for example, that there is a weak link between performance and investor-facing governance but a strong link between performance and an effectively functioning board.

Whether good corporate governance works must depend upon the constituency that is judging it. There are many interest groups and therefore the views each has of whether their particular interests are being served may vary widely.

Many scholars and consultants have attempted to measure whether governance improves financial returns to shareholders. Surveys by the consultants McKinsey & Co in 2000[19] and 2002[20] suggest it does, but survey evidence is indirect and unreliable. Respondents are self-selecting and the answers depend upon the questions asked. Respondents may have direct experience of costs, problems and inefficiencies but may have no better idea of their effects on performance than anyone else.

Newell and Wilson in 2002 compared 10 criteria for corporate governance with a measure of performance that used the ratio of share price to accounting-based book values.[21] Their results suggested a positive correlation.

Research from the Association of British Insurers (ABI),[22] based on 654 UK quoted companies, shows that those with the best corporate governance records, based on ABI chosen indicators, produced returns 18% higher than those with poor governance between 2003 and 2007. It suggests that each breach of best practice reduces a company's industry-adjusted return on assets by an average of 1% per year.

The research also shows that shareholders investing in a poorly governed company suffer from low returns. A sum of £100 invested in a company with no corporate governance problems leads to an average return of £120, but if invested in the worst governed companies the return would have been just £102.

Other key findings include:

● *The worst offending companies, which breached guidelines in every year examined, underperformed the average industry-adjusted return on assets by 3–5 percentage points a year. There was also found to be a time lag of two to three years between any breach and the impact on performance.*

[19] McKinsey and Co (2000) *Investor Opinion Survey*.

[20] McKinsey and Co (2002) *Global Investor Opinion Survey*.

[21] R Newell and G Wilson (2002) A premium for good governance, *McKinsey Quarterly*, (3), 20–23.

[22] '*Corporate governance "pays" for shareholders and company performance*', ABI News Release, 27 February 2008.

- *The volatility of share returns is 9% lower for well-governed companies than poorly governed companies.*
- *More non-executive directors on a board improves performance, though too great a number is linked to a fall in profitability.*
- *Companies that breached guidelines on shareholder pre-emption rights[23] showed a particularly large negative impact on performance, with an annual decrease of 3 percentage points of industry-adjusted ROA.*

Despite these findings, it remains difficult to prove the case conclusively. On the one hand, there are practical difficulties in defining and measuring good governance – once you define parameters, it may be hard to know which are more important; what if two parameters, taken together, are more than twice as effective as either on its own? On the other hand, there are problems defining performance when short-term profitability may be less relevant than the long-term's.

Good governance may be an insurance policy, with additional costs it incurs being an insurance premium and benefits perhaps accruing over a 10 or 20 year time horizon. Suppose, for example, that BA's problems in relation to price-fixing[24] would not have occurred or that GlaxoSmithKline's settlement with the FDA had not been necessary[25] if better corporate governance procedures were in place. These are pay-offs that may only occur once in 30 years, but the sums of money involved are very large.

There are other important issues; what of smaller or owner managed companies? Is the owner-manager protected by good governance? What effect is there on subordinates if directors or owners themselves behave badly? Studies, unsurprisingly, don't have the means to look directly at the effectiveness of the board itself and can only look at the form rather than the substance of governance. A company can apparently have the necessary systems and procedures, but they simply don't work because the necessary behaviours are not in place. So, Robert Maxwell recruited experienced and reputable non-executive directors to his Mirror Group but was able to overawe them in practice and, through appointing his sons to the company board, was able to pressure them so that he was able to remove funds from the company pension scheme to use, unlawfully, in supporting the company's own share price.[26]

Finally, there is the key question of whether compliance is the same thing as good governance. The head of corporate reporting for PwC has been reported as saying that compliance fatigue results from successive waves of ad hoc legislation, regulation and governance requirements. He also said that, 'the point

---

[23] Pre-emption is the right of existing shareholders to be offered shares in new issues to prevent their holdings being diluted.

[24] 'BA's price-fix fine reaches £270m', *BBC News*, 1 August 2007.

[25] FDA (2010) *GlaxoSmithKline Will Plead Guilty and Pay $750 Million to Resolve Manufacturing Deficiencies at Puerto Rico Plant*, press release, 26 October.

[26] Andreas Whittam Smith (2001) 'How Robert Maxwell picked the lock on the company safe', *The Independent*, 2 April.

has come where, if companies reported less, they would actually provide more insight and understanding'.[27] This is illustrated by the GSK case (p. 174) where the pages in the annual report devoted to listing business risks tick all the boxes but fail to give any real insight.

In conclusion, although it is hard to prove unequivocally that good governance leads to better performance, there is some suggestive data that it does. There is also evidence from disasters that suggests they may have been avoided by better governance.

Ian Hay Davison, former managing partner of Arthur Andersen and chairman of Lloyds of London said, 'Commenting on the [Cadbury] Report in 1993 I forecast that without legal sanctions it would be ineffective and would fail – I have been proved wrong: there have been profound changes in British boardrooms as a result of the Report and public attention in the last decade has focussed on the important area of corporate governance. Public exposure has brought about change – to borrow a phrase I used often at Lloyd's "sunshine drives away the mists".'[28]

Reasons for corporate social responsibility

In the introduction, I referred to Milton Friedman's view that the role of a company is solely to make profits. By extension, it can be argued that it is up to society, through its elected representatives, to set boundaries to the behaviour of individuals and organisations.

It has been said that companies do not exist in a vacuum but are vessels afloat on the sea of society. Their directors, employees, shareholders, suppliers and customers are also members of the community at large. They drink the water and breathe the air that their companies may also use to disperse waste products. So the employees of a brewery also suffer from the depradations of under-age drinkers; the directors of a tobacco company pay, through their taxes, for the ill-health of smokers; while shareholders in a fast food company also bear the costs of people who eat badly. At their extreme these are examples of the 'tragedy of the commons',[29] which results when 'multiple individuals, acting independently, and solely and rationally consulting their own self-interest, will ultimately deplete a shared limited resource even when it is clear that it is not in anyone's long-term interest for this to happen.'[30]

Advocates of CSR argue that companies should pursue, and report on, not just the 'bottom line' of profits but a 'triple bottom line' that includes environmental protection and social justice. It is hard enough for accountants and regulators

[27] PwC (2010) 'UK's leading companies suffer from "compliance fatigue" in their corporate reporting', press release, 1 October.

[28] 'Is Better Corporate Governance Working?', speech given by Ian Hay Davison at the ICAEW Trustee's Lecture, 18 October 2001.

[29] Garrett Hardin (1968) 'The tragedy of the commons', Science, **162**, 1243–1248.

[30] Wikipedia http://en.wikipedia.org/wiki/Tragedy_of_the_commons

to agree on how to report profits but, at least over the long term, all the different systems would converge: the other two targets are understood and valued differently by different parts of the community, so that defining and measuring them for reporting would be a major challenge. This may mean that 'a business that is accountable to all is in effect accountable to no one.'[31] Not for profit organisations such as Ceres[32] work with companies to try to find ways of dealing with these issues.

Most company directors would argue that it is not for them but for elected representatives to make difficult decisions on priorities and trade-offs and then to be accountable for their outcomes. They can see that many businesses produce externalities, using scarce resources or emitting pollutants whose consequences are not priced but are borne by the community. But company directors are neither elected by nor accountable to the community at large. Most would argue that difficult decisions, such as those that balance current needs against those of future generations, are not for them to make. If the law allows them to use scarce resources then they are entitled to do so.

 *If you have a responsibility, **make sure you know what it is and to whom it is owed**.*

If stopping dangerous disposal work locally means exporting it to the developing world, then that is merely transferring the problem to someone else. But subsequently removing that work from the developing world will remove the livelihoods of hundreds of families. Are company executives qualified and authorised to make these ethical decisions?

Companies and other organisations have the capacity to do harm, whether through environmental damage arising from disasters such as BP's Deepwater Horizon rig blowout (see page 151) or the spillage of toxic waste from aluminium processing in Hungary in 2010;[33] or arising from normal business practices such as mining, manufacturing or farming. The reality is that if companies do not take a proactive approach, then modern societies act against them. Governments seek ways to get businesses to police themselves through compliance with the law but also to get businesses to engage with the community in a positive way. Examples of society imposing responsibilities include equal pay, anti-discrimination, health and safety, anti-bribery, anti-money laundering, etc.

Governmental chivvying of companies is often done through imposing reporting requirements. Thus the Companies Act 2006 requires a business review that

[31] Ann Bernstein, head of the Centre for Development and Enterprise, quoted in 'Companies aren't charities, *The Economist,* 23–29 October 2010.

[32] www.ceres.org.

[33] Mark Tran and agencies (2010) 'Hungary toxic sludge spill an 'ecological catastrophe' says government', *Guardian.co.uk*, 5 October.

must, to the extent necessary for an understanding of the development, perform-ance or position of the company's business, include ...information about:

- *environmental matters (including the impact of the company's business on the environment)*
- *the company's employees, and*
- *social and community issues*

including

- *information about any policies of the company in relation to these matters and the effectiveness of those policies.*[34]

The Pensions Act Regulations require trustees of UK occupational pension funds to disclose in their Statement of Investment Principles 'the extent (if at all) to which social, environmental and ethical considerations are taken into account in the selection, retention and realisation of investments.'[35]

Companies that adopt CSR policies should use the same SMART principles set out under Managing meetings in Chapter 7. Directors must bear in mind that their principal duty is to the company albeit 'having regard to ... the impact of the company's operations on the community and the environment'[36] and must not use their position to promote their personal fads or beliefs at the expense of the company. They are custodians of the shareholders' money and it is not the place of directors or executives to spend it without good reason. The law only gets involved in respect of political donations in excess of £5,000, which must be authorised by a vote of members in general meeting.[37]

There are numerous examples where following socially responsible principles also has benefits for the company by enhancing its reputation, supporting its brand and reducing its costs, such as:

- Reducing inputs such as energy may reduce both carbon footprint and also costs.
- Reducing outputs such as waste may also reduce costs: for example, through reducing packaging.
- Following fair trade policies with respect to suppliers in developing countries may avert adverse publicity.

There is no clear distinction between these goals of CSR and what is described as 'sustainability'. The term is a relative one, meaning 'more sustain-

---

[34] Companies Act 2006 S417(5).

[35] Occupational Pension Schemes (Investment) Regulations 1996, S11A.

[36] Companies Act 2006 S172(1).

[37] ibid. Ss362–368, 378.

able', as in having less impact on the environment. The Brundtland Commission[38] defined it as:

> ... *development that meets the needs of the present without compromising the ability of future generations to meet their own needs.*[39]

But this would preclude any mining activity and therefore cannot be taken literally.

 The Times reported from the UN Climate Conference in Cancun that 'A group of consumer companies, headed by Paul Polman, of Unilever, and Sir Terry Leahy, of Tesco, used the conference to announce plans to cut deforestation and phase out refrigerant gases that add to global warming.'
However, they qualified this report by quoting 'one of the City's most powerful investors' as saying, 'Paul Polman would be on much stronger ground if Unilever's financial performance was better.'[40]

Briefing Lesson

● **The mass of investors wants good financial returns even more than they want corporate social responsibility.**

---

[38] World Commission on Environment and Development (WCED) convened by the UN in 1983 and reported in 1987. Was created to address concern 'about the accelerating deterioration of the human environment and natural resources and the consequences of that deterioration for economic and social development.'

[39] UN Brundtland Commission (1987) *Our Common Future*, Oxford Paperbacks, 43.

[40] David Wighton (2010) 'What's good for the planet is good for business', *The Times*, 1 December.

Who's doing it?
Who has done it?

4

Introduction and examples

A succession of reports on corporate governance has been commissioned or sponsored by the London Stock Exchange, the Financial Reporting Council, etc. These apply primarily to quoted companies but with the hope that there will be a trickle-down effect of improved governance to unquoted companies and to public bodies. All FTSE 350 companies and most large US corporations are required to have statements on corporate governance and CSR within their published accounts and on their websites, and many smaller companies also follow this as best practice. The QCA,[1] for example, sets a report from the chairman of how their guidelines are applied as a minimum disclosure requirement.

However, much of the compliance by big companies is not very informative, which may result from a box-ticking approach to detailed requirements. The QCA Guidelines takes a different approach from the Corporate Governance Code in establishing broad principles and leaving it to boards to think through how to comply. Tim Ward, QCA chief executive, quotes a company chairman telling him, 'It would be much easier if the QCA told me what to do rather than setting out principles.' But that is the point; by thinking through principles and using them to engage with shareholders and other stakeholder, the board can produce something more meaningful and more relevant.

An example of the 'boilerplate' approach from the Prudential plc website illustrates this:

> *As an international business, our objective is to apply consistently high standards throughout our operations wherever they are located, achieved through clear policies and effective governance. We believe that the result is socially acceptable business growth, bringing social and economic benefits to regions and locations and enhancing our ability to create and maintain market access for our products and services.*

What does that tell us? Lack of meaning is demonstrated by reversing the sentences. Would any business, for instance, have the objective of applying consistently **low** standards or espousing **unclear** policies and **ineffective** governance?

Nonetheless, the same site also illustrates clarity when it addresses sustainable development. Here, the ideas are expressed clearly, are specific, avoid vague generalities and talk about actions:

---

[1] The Quoted Companies Alliance represents small and mid-cap quoted companies.

Sustainable development

What's the issue?

The goal of sustainable development is to 'meet the needs of the present without compromising the ability of future generations to meet their own needs.'[2] Businesses have a role to play by managing their impact on the environment and in society.

What's happening?

International Agreements such as the Rio Earth Summit and Kyoto have seen nations taking action to mitigate impacts such as global warming.

Climate change is one of the most significant issues facing us all today. Through the consumption of fossil fuels for heating, electricity generation and transportation, CO_2 emissions contribute to global warming. The precise effects of climate change as a result of global warming cannot be predicted, but they already include changing weather patterns, extreme weather conditions and the possibility of sudden and irreversible step shifts in climatic patterns.

The Johannesburg Summit in 2002 extended considerations more widely to look at social issues, with the development of social action programmes. One of these areas related to sustainable consumption, which encompasses the concepts of consumer protection and education, in order that individuals can make informed judgements on the relative performance of products and services.

The challenge in a nutshell?

Natural resources are not unlimited and it is essential that businesses manage their environmental impact efficiently. But sustainable development is about more than reducing the consumption of raw materials and limiting negative environmental impact. It also means: ensuring human rights, treating customers, employees and service providers fairly, providing consumer education, and acting responsibly towards the communities in which we operate.

As a responsible business, we seek to ensure that we understand issues of sustainable development and direct our efforts to those that can be most effectively targeted.

Climate change – our position

We are committed to reducing our environmental impact including our carbon dioxide emissions and have been committed to reducing our impact for some

[2] UN Brundtland Commission (1987) *Our Common Future*, Oxford Paperbacks, 43.

time. There are various ways that companies can reduce their impact, like off-setting, but we intend to introduce a carbon management programme based on reduction before we consider the prospect of carbon offsetting.

We are focused on reducing our direct emissions, reducing the carbon footprint of our business operations and creating bottom-line savings by implementing cost effective energy efficiency measures and, where cost-effective, reducing the carbon intensity of our energy supply.

It is also our policy to work in partnership with our suppliers to help them reduce their impact, thereby indirectly reducing ours.

ClimateWise principles

Prudential is one of 38 companies from the financial services sector to endorse the ClimateWise principles, launched on 13 September 2007. The principles have been developed by leading global insurers, reinsurers, brokers and asset managers to promote action on climate change. They will enable companies and organisations throughout the world to build climate change into their business operations.

The principles have been developed by a working group led by the Association of British Insurers and focus on: encouraging greater climate-friendly behaviour among customers and employees; integrating climate change into investment strategies and risk analysis.

Pearson Group plc, owner of the publisher of this book, is a FTSE 100 company and therefore subject to the Code. Its 2009 annual report and accounts is a well-written, instructive document that complies rather than explaining why it does not observe provisions except for arguing in favour of continuing to retain the services of a non-executive director who has served more than nine years. However, even a company like this can be faulted. For example:

- It does not seem to comply with the Code provision calling for non-executive directors to be 'offered the opportunity to attend scheduled meetings with shareholders'[3] but does not explain its non-compliance.
- There is little detail of any continuing development for directors, although board presentations may contribute to this. The sentence that 'externally run courses are made available if directors wish to make use of them' resonates of a tick-box approach.
- The report of an extensive programme for executive directors and senior managers to meet institutional shareholders is impressive but contrasts with a more passive approach towards engagement by non-executive directors.

[3] Corporate Governance Code SE.1.1.

- The nature and diversity of Pearson's businesses seems to give rise to fewer potentially catastrophic risks than, say, a chemicals company, a drugs company or an airline might face. However, they still feel obliged to include three pages on the principal risks facing the business, which is so general that it leaves the reader not much wiser.

Nonetheless most company reports provide much more extensive information than would have been available in the past.

What do success and failure look like?

To differentiate success and failure we must compare outcomes with objectives (see What is it for? in Chapter 2) . These objectives fall into three main areas:

- accountability
- balancing interests
- effective management.

Accountability refers to a wide range of stakeholders and not just shareholders, so it includes:

- compliance with laws and regulations
- timely and adequate information to enable stakeholders to make informed decisions
- processes to enable stakeholders to exercise their rights.

Balancing interests mainly applies to potential differences between management and shareholders, but it will also have to take account of employees and the wider society. It will include:

- avoidance of conflicts of interest
- management of reputation
- communication.

Effective management is a key objective of good governance because the most obvious consequence of failure is corporate damage. It therefore includes issues such as:

- risk management
- effective systems and procedures
- independent voices on the board.

Successes and failures of corporate governance are summed up in Table 4.1.

Table 4.1 Success and failure of corporate governance

Success	Failure
Has clear and fair procedures and an effective board and management *Procedures are clearly documented from the board level down and their workings are re-examined periodically and amended if necessary.*	**Directors or senior employees derive unfair advantage from the company** *The remuneration policy for directors and senior executives may be excessive or unrelated to performance. Severance payments appear unduly generous.*
Complies with relevant laws and regulations and with best practice *This applies throughout the organisation and not just at board level. For directors to say they 'did not know' about the failings of their subordinates will reflect a breakdown of corporate governance.*	**Conflicts of interest are apparent** *The Company's directors may have personal interests in other companies with which they do business.*
Is open, honest and transparent in its dealings *This means full and accurate disclosure to shareholders to enable them to make informed decisions but also to other stakeholders. The company also discusses how it applies governance procedures.*	**Non-executive directors have many other directorships** *They have insufficient time to devote to the business.*
Avoids conflicts of interests *In the event of a conflict emerging there are clear procedures and individuals involved recuse themselves from taking part in the decision.*	**Internal conflicts arise between directors, and between functional areas and layers of the organisation hierarchy**
Sincere efforts are made to balance stakeholder interests	**Individuals who try to report matters of concern are victimised** *Whistleblowing procedures either don't exist or are unpublicised or are distrusted by staff.*
	Direction and control by the board are ineffective If good policies are espoused by the board but are not applied further down the organisation then this represents a failure of governance. ▶

Table 4.1 Success and failure of corporate governance *continued*

Success	Failure
Has clearly stated values that are observed throughout the company *Companies that have good governance will usually pursue effective CSR policies, not because they are required or politically correct but because they are a genuine element of their brand.*	**There is a high degree of secrecy, lack of communication or misleading communication**
	Risks are inadequately managed *The evidence for this is that disasters occur but even before that the use of bland and meaningless statements in company communications may be a warning sign.*
Communicates its values to all employees, business partners and stakeholders *The language is not of vague generalities but is clear and understandable. It ensures that the governance template established by the board is carried out by the organisation.*	**Company employees behave in an illegal or unethical manner, resulting in fines or reputational damage**
There are no scandals *There may be errors and mistakes but no scandals because there are checks and balances and open communication.*	**The manifest corporate culture is toxic to employees and business partners** *When bullying, discrimination, selfish and untrustworthy behaviour are manifest within an organisation, this is usually due to a failure of governance.*

PART TWO

In practice

The issues discussed here have often been developed with particular application to large corporate bodies, but the same broad principles generally apply to all companies. Clearly an owner-managed business will have differences but, if it has any outside shareholders, there will be potential conflicts of interest to manage and there will be potential differences between directors to be managed. Such a business will still benefit from outside experience and from an independent voice in key decisions. As private companies grow and develop, so their governance issues also change and grow.

How to do it: role and duties of directors

5

Introduction

What is the role of the board and of an individual director and how is that the same as or different from the role of senior executives? First, there is no single code of law or regulation that defines these things. For the first time, British law has codified some elements in the 2006 Companies Act, but even here it is setting boundaries rather than prescribing detailed governance requirements. The board and its members have two broad functions. They:

- **direct** – literally setting the direction of the company. This about goals, policies and strategies.
- **supervise** – monitoring and establishing control systems to ensure that their direction is implemented and check that operational management performs as required.

The UK has a unitary board system, unlike many continental European countries, which have a supervisory board for large companies as well, made up entirely of non-executive directors, including employee representatives. This contrasts with the UK system where directors owe their duty to the company and not specifically to its shareholders nor to any other interest group. This model means that directors usually also have an executive role, so they must manage departments or functions within the organisation as well as directing it from the board. The argument in favour of this system is that those who direct bring to bear real hands-on experience and deep understanding of the business.

The UK Companies Act 2006 confirms the common law position that a director's duty is to the company. It is not to shareholders nor to a particular shareholder who appointed that director but to the company. What does that mean? A useful illustration is provided by Professor Bob Garratt[1] who cites an East Asian group of companies, listed on a local exchange, but with a major multinational shareholder listed in London and New York. He reports that during the 1997 Asian financial crisis the multinational demanded a cash transfer from the Asian company, which may have left it short of cash. The local directors, possibly appointed at the behest of the multinational, complied. UK law is clear: if a transfer is contrary to the interests of the company then directors would be in breach of their duties for allowing it. This would be true even if the company receiving the funds held a majority stake.

This is a particularly difficult but important issue where companies have complex and interlinking shareholdings. Although these structures are rare in the UK, they are particularly common in Asia and some Continental European countries, where they maintain family control or reinforce trading relationships. For example, the Agnelli family in Italy maintains effective control of Fiat despite directly owning relatively few shares in the company. In extreme cases, such

[1] Bob Garratt (2006) '*Why Corporate Governance Matters and How to Measure and Improve Board Performance*', (2nd edn), Nicholas Brealey.

cross-holdings by companies can mean that outside shareholders have little influence and there is little real accountability.

What is meant by having a duty to the company? The seminal court case *Salomon* v *Salomon* established the principle that a company is a legal personality separate from its shareholders. The consequence of this is that directors are entitled to pursue the long-term interests of the company even if that is at the expense of short-term profits. This may prefer the interests of future shareholders to those of present shareholders and the only recourse the former have is to vote the directors out of office.

> *The directors are not servants to obey directions given by the shareholders as individuals; they are not agents appointed by and bound to serve the shareholders as their principles. They are persons who may by the regulations be entrusted with the control of the business, and if so entrusted they can be dispossessed from that control only by the statutory majority which can alter the articles. Directors are not, I think, bound to comply with the directions even of all the corporators acting as individuals.*[2]

The Companies Act 2006 codified directors' duties[3]

1 To act in accordance with the company's constitution and only exercise powers for the purpose they are conferred
2 To promote the success of the company
3 To exercise independent judgement
4 To use reasonable care, skill and diligence
5 To avoid conflicts of interest
6 Not to accept benefits from third parties
7 To declare an interest in a proposed transaction or arrangement.

In certain circumstances, breaches of these duties may be ratified by shareholders even, for private companies, by directors who do not have a conflict of interest.

The duty to use reasonable care, skill and diligence calls for some further explanation. The Act sets two requirements for the director:

- 'To display the knowledge, skill and experience'
    a. '...that may reasonably be expected of a person carrying out [those] functions'
    b. '...that the director has'

---

[2] Lord Justice Buckley, *The Gramophone and Typewriter Ltd* v *Stanley*, 1908.
[3] Companies Act 2006 S171–177.

- So, 'A private company appoints a qualified accountant as its marketing director and an unqualified person as its finance director. The marketing director will be expected to exercise the skill of a qualified accountant in all aspects of decision-making. The finance director will be expected the skill of a reasonable finance director and will not be excused any lack of skill because they are, in fact, unqualified.'[4]

For the first time, the Companies Act established the principle in British law that directors must consider stakeholders and not just shareholder interests. It states that a director must act in a way that he considers in good faith would be most likely to promote the success of the company for the benefit of its members as a whole, and in doing so have regard (amongst other matters) to:

a. *the likely consequences of any decision in the long-term,*
b. *the interests of the company's employees,*
c. *the need to foster business relationships with suppliers customers, and others,*
d. *the impact of the company's operations on the community and the environment,*
e. *the desirability of the company maintaining a reputation for high standards of business conduct and*
f. *the need to act fairly as between members of the company.*[5]

The government did not anticipate that this change would have much impact on well-run companies, which would be considering these factors anyway; but there was, nonetheless, concern that it would lead to increase documentation and an unproductive box-ticking approach. During the passage of the Bill, Attorney General, Lord Goldsmith, said in the Lords:

There is nothing in this Bill that says there is a need for a paper trail.… I do not agree that the effect of passing this Bill will be that directors will be subject to a breach if they cannot demonstrate that they have considered every element. It will be for the person who is asserting breach of duty to make that case good… [Derivative claims] will be struck out if there is no decent basis for them.[6]

The GC100 Group, representing company secretaries and legal officers of FTSE100 companies, has published guidance[7] on best practice that argues that, since the requirement is only to take decisions having regard to these matters, it can be satisfied in ways that are not onerous. These can be summarised as a three-stage process:

[4] David Chivers QC (2004) *The Companies Act 2006: Directors Duties Guidance*, The Corporate Responsibility Coalition, 11.

[5] Companies Act 2006 S172(1).

[6] Hansard, 9 May 2006: col 841

[7] GC100 Group (2007) *Companies Act (2006) – Directors' duties*, 7 February.

- ensuring directors understand their responsibilities
- delegating detailed consideration to the management team
- having adequate board papers as background to board discussions.

It should therefore be best practice for those members of the management team responsible for preparing the paper to ensure that each of the relevant factors, including those referred to in the Companies Act, are properly considered whilst the paper is being prepared. They can then, if necessary, be included in the paper or any presentation made. Responsibility for considering relevant factors can properly be delegated to the members of the management team preparing the paper in the usual way. In some cases, one or more particular factors may clearly be irrelevant....[and] GC100 does not believe that best practice should be prescriptive by requiring a negative statement.[8]

Board minutes ... are ... a summary and can never ... be prepared with the thoroughness of a board paper. In some cases, companies have very brief minutes, for example, where there is a specific need to avoid detailed references to legal advice to ensure privilege is not lost. It is therefore recommended that board minutes should not be used as the main medium for recording the extent to which each of the factors of the Companies Act were discussed.[9]

Since directors' primary responsibility is to the company, if the company's interests demanded decisions that were lawful but detrimental, say, to the environment, these provisions would seem no impediment to taking such a decision.

Directors' responsibilities to the company can be over-ridden – they are 'subject to any enactment or rule of law requiring directors, in certain circumstances, to consider or act in the interests of creditors of the company.'[10] If a company is in financial difficulties, there comes a point where the directors' duties shift to protecting creditors' interests. It is easy to envisage circumstances where shareholders' equity may have become worthless and directors may be tempted to take an extreme business risk in order to recover some or all of its value. Since shareholders have nothing left to lose, it would then be the creditors who may, unwittingly, be taking the financial risk.

In these circumstances a director can become personally liable if a company goes into insolvent liquidation[11] and the rights of creditors have been ignored through wrongful trading. Directors should take detailed legal advice in such circumstances.

[8] ibid. S6.3 (c), (d).
[9] ibid. S6.3 (f).
[10] Companies Act 2006 S172(3).
[11] Insolvency Act 1986 S214.

Limiting liability of directors

A company cannot directly protect its directors from their liabilities resulting from negligence, default, breach of duty or trust; but it may do so indirectly through the use of insurance. It may also provide a director with an indemnity against third parties. This may not apply to fines or regulatory penalties nor to the costs of defending civil or criminal proceedings where the court finds against the director.[12]

Director development

The principles of the Code that relate to the induction, training and development of directors are absolutely applicable to companies of every type and size and should be best practice for all. Its main principle is that 'All directors should receive induction on joining the board and should regularly update and refresh their skills and knowledge.'[13] Induction, in particular, should include developing understanding of all areas of the company's business and familiarity with its key locations and markets as well as knowing its senior executives. Whilst non-executive directors will need a different induction experience from those promoted from within, even someone who has worked in the business for a long time may not be familiar with aspects outside their functional specialism.

According to the Institute of Company Secretaries and Administrators (ICSA), the induction should include:[14]

- **Board matters**
    - duties and responsibilities
    - board procedures, including matters delegated and those reserved for board decision
    - delegated authority
    - the policy for directors to obtain independent advice
    - the company Memorandum and Articles of Association
    - recent board minutes
    - key dates of future board meetings, announcements, etc.
    - brief biographical and contact details of directors, company secretary and key executives; contact details of the company's advisers
    - details of board committees and their terms of reference
- **Company business**
    - outline of company history
    - recent business plans, budgets, forecasts, statutory and management accounts
    - explanation of key performance indicators

[12] Companies Act 2006 Ss232–234.

[13] Corporate Governance Code SB.4.

[14] Extracted from ICSA (2003) *Guidance Note: Induction of Directors*.

- details of actual or potential litigation
- treasury issues: funding, covenants, etc.
- corporate brochures, mission statements, etc.
- risk management procedures and disaster recovery plans
- details of largest and critical customers and suppliers.

The Code states that induction and development needs should be overseen by the chairman following agreement with each director. It also says directors should 'avail themselves of opportunities to meet major shareholders', presumably for the benefit of the shareholders as much as the directors.

For some individuals, short courses through business schools may be helpful, and the Institute of Directors runs a Chartered Director programme, which has had nearly 7,000 people pass through it. These can all be valuable tools, but Sir Adrian Cadbury's caveat is wise. He notes that there is no generally accepted corpus of knowledge, skills and experience required for being a successful board director and observes that 'investors are looking for directors who will take intelligent risks and grow their businesses, not for successful exam takers.'[15]

Qualification for directors

Qualifications to hold a directorship are only required in three instances:

1 By age, a director must be over the age of 16.
2 For companies regulated by the FSA which enforces the requirement for directors of investment companies to be 'fit and proper persons'.[16] The FSA approves individuals as fit and proper to carry out duties, including those of a director for a controlled firm (one that carries out investment activities). It has been taking a much more active role in interviewing directors, and particularly non-executives, before approval and, on a sample basis, to maintain this status. Whilst the FSA guidelines, published in 2004, specify the individual's honesty, integrity and reputation, on the one hand, and competence, on the other, reports from interviewees shows the questioning of non-executive directors appears to focus on whether the individual can demonstrate a record, an ability and a willingness to pose probing questions and to challenge the executives where necessary. Whether these interviews have resulted in the disapproval of existing directors is not clear, but the intent is clear: to ensure that, at least for financial services companies, their boards really do hold the executive branch to account effectively.
3 At least one real person must be a director and then there can be companies fulfilling the role.[17]

[15] Sir Adrian Cadbury (2002) *Corporate Governance and Chairmanship*, Oxford University Press, 207.

[16] Financial Services and Markets Act 2000, S61.

[17] Companies Act 2006 S155.

There are a number of ways in which someone can be disqualified from being a company director:

- A bankrupt cannot be a company director.
- The courts may disqualify a director for misconduct.
- The DTI or official receiver can apply to the courts to declare that a director of an insolvent company is unfit to be concerned in management.[18]
- Someone who fails to pay under a county court administration order may be disqualified from being a company director.[19]

A person may also be disqualified indirectly if the Gambling Commission deems them not 'fit and proper'. In that case, the company of which they were a director would be unable to carry on its gambling business.

Removal of directors

Any company director can be removed from office by a simple majority vote at a general meeting, and the resolution to propose removal can be put forward by any shareholders holding more than 5% of the ordinary shares by value. The individual may be entitled to compensation under a service contract.

Articles of a company can usually provide other means of removing a director. For example, a start-up business had been largely funded by an investor who also became a director and its Articles provided for him to be able to remove any of the other directors as long as he had a majority of the shares. The directors' individual contracts can also specify termination rights. The model articles provided under S19 of the Companies Act 2006 also provide causes for automatic termination, including being physically or mentally incapable of acting as a director, becoming bankrupt or making a composition with creditors.[20]

Conflicts of interest

Conflict of interest refers to any transaction or decision where an executive or director, their friends or family, who will influence the outcome will derive a potential benefit or loss. There are obvious ones:

- entering into transactions with another organisation in which the director or executive has an interest
- being party to deciding your own remuneration, benefits or loan arrangements

---

[18] Company Directors Disqualification Act 1986 as amended by the Insolvency Act 2000.
[19] ibid.
[20] The Companies (Model Articles) Regulations 2008, S18.

- insider dealing (see below) and, particularly for private companies,
- buying or selling assets from or to directors or companies they are associated with.

But there are more complex ones too:

- negotiating a company sale or reorganisation that would cost your own job or status or, conversely, lead to a better job
- pursuing strategies that may enhance management status or ego but may not be in the interests of shareholders – academic research suggests that the majority of corporate acquisitions end up destroying shareholder value
- merely having been appointed at the behest of one of the shareholders whose interests may diverge from those of other shareholders.

Directors have a duty under the Companies Act to avoid conflicts of interest.[21] The failure of a director to declare an interest in a transaction is a criminal offence and the interested director must not count towards a quorum or vote on the transaction.[22]

A conflict can be authorised by the board of a private company, provided there is nothing in the Articles to prevent it. For a public company, there must be a term in its Articles to permit the board to authorise the conflict.

Shareholder approval is required to authorise conflicts such as substantial transactions with directors to buy or sell property[23] or, unless in the ordinary course of business, to make loans to directors or provide security for loans.[24]

The FSA separately requires[25] listed companies to obtain shareholder approval for related party transactions if the transaction value represents more than 5% of its gross assets, profits or gross capital. For values between 0.25% and 5%, then it is sufficient to notify the FSA through an independent adviser that the transaction is fair and reasonable and details must be published in the next report and accounts.

Directors' share dealings

For listed companies, Persons Discharging Managerial Duties (PDMD) must notify their company within four days of all transactions in shares, derivatives or other market instruments.[26] This applies also to 'connected persons' who are defined in the Companies Act as family members, trustees, partners, corporate

[21] Companies Act 2006 S175.

[22] ibid. 175(6).

[23] ibid. S188.

[24] ibid. S197.

[25] *FSA Handbook*, Listing Rule 11.1.

[26] *FSA Handbook*, Market Abuse Directive 2005, Article 6(4).

bodies in which the individual has a financial interest, etc.[27] The company must then notify the market by the end of the next business day.

Directors' dealings include not just buying or selling but pledging shares for a loan, lending shares or granting an option.

 On 8 December 2008 David Ross, co-founder of quoted company Carphone Warehouse, resigned from the board when it emerged that he had pledged his £157m of shares to secure a loan for his property empire but had failed to disclose this to the company. The Times *reported[28] the following day that he was under investigation by the FSA.*

In January 2009 the Telegraph *reported[29] the FSA announcement of an amnesty covering Ross and company directors in a similar position as long as disclosures were made within two weeks. The reason given was uncertainty in the framing of the EU Market Abuse Directive leading to different practices across Europe, although UK law seems to have been clear all along.*

A company has an obligation to notify the market, as soon as practical, of any information which would be likely to lead to substantial movement in the price of its shares.

 Definition

For quoted companies, the Listing Rules define a close period when no dealing in securities is allowed. This is:

- **60 days before the preliminary announcement of results, and**
- **60 days before their publication**
- **and, for quarterly and half year reports it is from the period end to publication.**

In addition, there is a ban on dealing when a person has inside information. This applies to directors and senior executives who have 'regular access to inside information' and have 'power to make managerial decisions affecting … future development and business prospects.'[30]

For dealings outside the close period, individuals must get clearance from the chairman or, as is normal, the chairman's nominated director/officer which, in practice, is usually the company secretary. These various restrictions also apply to connected persons.

[27] Companies Act 2006 Ss252–254.

[28] Dan Sabbagh, Lily Peel, Jill Sherman and Helen Power (2008) 'Carphone Warehouse founder David Ross quits in disgrace over secret share deals', *The Times*, 9 December.

[29] Katherine Griffiths (2009) 'FSA gives directors amnesty', *The Telegraph*, 9 Jan.

[30] Financial Services and Markets Act 2000, S96B.

Integrity and values

It is impossible to discuss governance meaningfully without including integrity and values. This is because regulations and codes of practice are all very well but these too can be subverted without goodwill. Consider some practical examples.

In 2007 Lehman Brothers, headquartered in New York, collapsed and its failure caused a severe jolt to the world's financial system because of its size and hugely complicated web of dealings with other banks around the world. It quickly became public that the bank had used devices known as Repo 105 and Repo 108 at the end of reporting periods in order to enable it to omit some $50bn of borrowing from its published balance sheets. But after the initial shock of this revelation there was a second shock as it became clear that this procedure was probably legal. Bank executives had taken advantage of the US rules-based regulatory system to comply with rules whilst simultaneously presenting a totally misleading picture to its investors and bankers.

The earlier Enron collapse in 2001 displayed some similar characteristics. A huge public company had used complex schemes that appear to have complied with the law and accounting rules and yet presented a misleading picture of its finances. In this case we know, from published investigations, that, while the board seems to have been unaware of some of what was going on, they were aware of at least one of these schemes, whose sole purpose was to mislead – not to create economic benefit – and they authorised at least one that gave rise to a blatant conflict of interest for the company's chief financial officer.

Once you cross the ethical line, you advertise to your subordinates that such behaviour is tolerated and it becomes harder to prevent them doing similar things without authority; it also becomes difficult to prevent actions that go a little further and then a little further.

Although these examples are drawn from the USA, it would be a mistake to imagine that such problems do not occur elsewhere. Virtually every company that reports its financial results will delay payments to creditors that are due on or before its record date and pay them a few days later. This results in showing lower borrowing (or higher cash reserves) than is actually normal for the business. How big a step is it from there to something a little worse?

There is a witty, if apparently cynical, view of the ethical behaviour of boards from author, Nell Minow: 'boards of directors are like subatomic particles–they behave differently when they are observed.'[31] But of course we all behave differently when observed and this is not always conscious. The point is that we are more likely to resist temptation as well as external pressure when we are under scrutiny, which is why legislators and others focus so much on transparency as a corporate governance tool.

[31] Robert Monks and Nell Minow (1992) *Power and Accountability*. Harper Collins, 288.

How to do it: role and duties of the board

6

Introduction

What is a company board of directors for?

> '...management runs the business; the board ensures that it is being well run and run in the right direction.'[1]

The historical perspective helps through showing how we got here. The early business models had individual traders who might come together as partners in particular ventures. So, for example, the Medici Bank, in fifteenth century Florence was a partnership, or rather a series of partnerships since its branches in different cities had different, generally family, partners. In this way, larger sums of capital could be raised and management ability rewarded. Jumping forward to seventeenth century England, the East India Company was given a royal charter or monopoly on a particular area of trade which, like a patent, was to ensure that the benefits of investing in a high-risk venture would not simply accrue to other merchants who would follow. There were too many investors to each take part in managing the enterprise and so there was the equivalent of a board of directors who would manage and also account to the investors for the results.

The modern board shares these functions but also acts as a group mind to direct the activities of the business. Through discussion and debate, it should come up with better decisions overall than one person on their own would.

The British legal system barely deals with the role of the board, but focuses on individual directors, their appointment, removal, powers and duties to shareholders. Who sits on a board, what it does and how it organises itself are left to companies themselves to arrange. The roles of chairman and managing director are not defined except to the extent that a chairman chairs a board meeting. As far as the law is concerned, the board could appoint a different chairman at each meeting.

However, custom and practice together with codes of governance have developed expectations about the board and how it should be run.

Basic functions of the board

The key roles of the board are to:

- direct
- supervise
- decide its members and order its proceedings
- communicate.

[1] Bob Tricker (2009) *Corporate Governance: Principles, Policies and Practices*, Oxford University Press, 36.

Direct

This covers setting goals and originating or approving strategy. It can also cover setting values, organisational vision and leadership.

The Code establishes two other duties under this heading:

- **To agree their appetite for risk**

'The board is responsible for determining the nature and extent of significant risks it is willing to take in achieving its strategic objectives.'[2]

- **To monitor risks**

'The board should maintain sound risk management and internal control systems.'[3]

Although small companies are exempt, other companies must include a business review in the directors' report which must, inter alia, contain a 'description of the principle risks and uncertainties facing the company.'[4]

Supervise

This means that the board should implement adequate systems to ensure that employees pursue the goals and strategies set by the board and adhere to its vision and values and to control day-to-day management.

In addition to maintaining risk management and control systems, the Code states that:

'The board should, at least annually, conduct a review of the effectiveness of the company's risk management and internal control systems and should report to shareholders that they have done so. The review should cover all material controls, including financial, operational and compliance controls.'[5]

Whilst being less prescriptive, both the QCA (for smaller listed companies) and the Institute of Directors (for unlisted companies) recognise the centrality of internal control and risk management.

Decide its members and order its proceedings

Although shareholders must approve directors and, occasionally, will vote out or vote in their own candidates, normally the members of the board are appointed

---

[2] Corporate Governance Code SC.2.
[3] Corporate Governance Code SC.2.
[4] Companies Act 2006 S413(3)(b).
[5] Corporate Governance Code SC.2.1.

by the board. It will also often approve the appointment of senior operational management. In addition the board decides its own procedures.

Communicate

The board has a threefold communications role:

- shareholders
- other external stakeholders
- internal.

'The board as a whole has responsibility for ensuring that a satisfactory dialogue with shareholders takes place.'[6] In practice, this duty is normally split three ways, with the chairman, chief executive and finance director all taking a role. There are no rules governing how they decide to divide these responsibilities, although the CEO and finance director will normally meet stockbrokers' analysts whilst the chairman or CEO will be the main contacts for large shareholders. The Code provides for a senior independent director to 'be available to shareholders if they have concerns which contact through the normal channels …has failed to resolve or…is inappropriate.'[7]

 Tip

This role overlaps with supervision, particularly in the realm of financial reporting to shareholders.

Such critical decisions about the basis of reporting and the future of a business are, in this case, inextricable from the communication role. Another example arises from an acquisition or a bid from an outside party, when the Takeover Code requires the entire board to take responsibility for circulars to shareholders (see Takeovers in Chapter 9).

The board is the public face of a company, communicating with authorities, financial institutions, community interests, customers and suppliers. This role is generally handled, in practice, by the chairman or chief executive, but the board will normally retain oversight.

Internal communication is managed by the executive team, but it is a derogation of responsibility for a board to abdicate oversight of this, since the implementation of governance procedures depend upon it. The role of the board

[6] ibid. SE1.
[7] ibid. SA.4.1.

in setting the corporate values and vision is also indissolubly linked to communicating them.

In the UK, directors often have a dual role as functional managers: so they are both the controllers and the controlled. This is a characteristic of the UK's unitary board system, which contrasts with some continental European countries' systems of supervisory boards. These appoint members of the management board and have the final say in major decisions: they perform, essentially, a monitoring function. It is also rather different from the US unitary board system that primarily has members from outside the company but is often dominated by a CEO who also holds the chairmanship. This individual manages the board, controls the agenda and the flow of information as well as being in charge of the operations of the company. It is a far more centralised system, with the board largely performing a monitoring role but often only coming to the fore in a crisis when it may remove the CEO. Two-tier and unitary sysyems are compared in Table 6.1.

Table 6.1 Advantages of unitary versus two-tier board

Advantages of two-tier board	Advantages of unitary system
Allows formal stakeholder representation	Faster decision-making
Ensures an independent control of executive management	Cheaper system
Provides a clear separation for monitoring and management functions	Functional expertise informs board decisions
	Input of day-to-day issues
	The board can easily quiz senior management

The board may delegate some of its authority to sub-committees or to specific executives who may or may not be board members. Ian Hay Davison recommends that there should be a board minute recording what is delegated and what is reserved for the board as a whole to deal with.[8]

Size of the board

There is no ideal size of board except that larger ones tend to result in the formation of an inner circle. The board needs to be large enough to provide a mix of experience and skills yet small enough that its members can get to know each other and can engage in proper discussion and debate. The Code specifies having at least 50% non-executive directors (or at least two for small companies).

[8] 'Is Better Corporate Governance Working?', speech given by Ian Hay Davison at the ICAEW Trustees' Lecture, 18 October 2001.

After considering recommendations of different writers, Sir Adrian Cadbury thinks a limit of around ten seems about right. Between 8 and 12 members is probably about right from the viewpoint of group dynamics; beyond this size, a group is likely to sub-divide into smaller groups. However, this size also raises a problem of composition.

Composition of the board

The Code is not prescriptive about the composition of the board, instead calling for:

- At least half the board, excluding the chairman, to comprise independent non-executive directors.[9]
- 'The board and its committees [to] have the appropriate balance of skills, experience, independence and knowledge of then company to enable them to discharge their respective duties and responsibilities effectively.'[10]
- Appointments to be made 'on merit, against objective criteria and with due regard for the benefits of diversity'.[11]

Smaller companies may not have the resources for such formal systems, though the Code calls for at least two independent non-executive directors for smaller companies. The principles for all organisations should be to:

- appoint people with a mix of skills and backgrounds and not just clones of one type and not just friends of a dominant director
- appoint people who can provide different perspectives and contribute to better decisions
- decide what skills and characteristics (including personality) are required and then seek the people to match them: don't choose the person first.

Chairmen have to be resolute in agreeing to the appointment of executives to the board, not on grounds of seniority nor as a reward for service, but on their merits as potential directors.[12]

The requirement for 50% of the board to comprise non-executives gives a problem. If a board includes the main skills areas for most companies – chief executive, operations, marketing, finance, human resources – then, balanced by independent non-executive directors and adding a chairman already gives 11

[9] Corporate Governance Code SB.1.2.
[10] ibid. SB.1.
[11] ibid. SB.2.
[12] Sir Adrian Cadbury (2002) *Corporate Governance and Chairmanship*.

people before addressing particular roles peculiar to individual companies, which might merit representation. If important roles are excluded, then the non-executives may have limited access to information on those areas. One solution may be for companies to have senior executives regularly present at board meetings ex-officio to present reports and be available for questions. Alternatives include formal briefing sessions to the board by functional and business heads. But there is always the option to over-ride the Code requirement if it proves impractical.[13]

Many businesses have executive committees that may meet informally or formally, minuted or not. These will often comprise individuals not represented on the main board. It may be useful for non-executive directors, in particular, to have access to senior executives who are members of such committees.

The focus on skill sets calls for a wide range of skills and experience at board level but the tendency amongst listed companies is to restrict this to individuals who have had main board experience on other listed companies, which limits the available pool for recruitment. This probably contributes to the low levels of representation of women and minorities amongst non-executive directors. Little seems to have changed since 2003 when the Higgs Report and the Tyson Report on the Recruitment and Development of Non-Executive Directors[14] both advocated the business benefits of board diversity. Laura Tyson recommended casting the net for recruitment more widely, to include people whose experience had been just below board level as well as considering those whose experience came from being consultants or advisers to businesses.

Concerned about the slow rate of progress towards gender equality on boards, the UK government commissioned a report from Lord Davies which reported in February 2011.[15] Although press reports had indicated he might recommend quotas, the outcome was a recommendation for FTSE 100 companies to aim for 25% female board representation by 2015; with FTSE 350 companies invited to set themselves a more challenging target; and for headhunting firms to draw up a voluntary code of practice addressing gender diversity in relation to board level appointments to FTSE 350 companies. Behind all this exhortation there is an implication of legislation if the voluntary approach does not work. Meanwhile, the EU justice commissioner has said that quotas, backed by legal instruments, might be necessary if businesses don't start to comply voluntarily.

Many director positions occupied by women are non-executive. The real problem is therefore gender equality in the senior executive roles. This requires changing attitudes to flexible careers, flexible working and career breaks and not government action that may encourage either more female non-executive directors or more roles for each one.

---

[13] ICSA (2009) *'Boardroom Behaviours'*, S2.12.

[14] Laura Tyson (2003) *The Tyson Report on the Recruitment and Development of Non-Executive Directors*, London Business School.

[15] Lord Davies (2011) *Women on Boards*, Department for Business, Innovation and Skills.

Quorum, meetings by telephone, etc.

When urgent and significant issues arise outside the normal schedule for board meetings, it is important to have procedures in place for information to be supplied to all directors, for meetings to be convened at short notice and for participation via telephone or internet links. Companies' Articles of Association may need to be amended to permit telephone meetings and possibly to ensure that quorum requirements can be met. It is important, though, to avoid excluding directors from key decisions through using small-quorum meetings: every effort must be made to include all directors even in respect of urgent issues.

For international and private companies that may have less frequent board meetings, such arrangements may be especially appropriate, especially to deal with crises that may require almost daily meetings.

Non-executive directors

The role of non-executive directors is not to add a veneer of legitimacy to businesses nor to support the chairman. It has, after all, been noted that the law makes no distinction between the duties and liabilities of executive and non-executive directors, and so trophy directors who do not take their role seriously run a serious risk of incurring personal liabilities through negligence as well as damage to their reputation.

It is important that the person who takes on this role is committed to the company and is able to devote sufficient time to it to fulfil their responsibilities.[16]

The purposes of having NEDs are:

- to bring in wider experience and different viewpoints
- to introduce an independent view of business issues
- to balance a dominant director
- to take a lead where potential conflicts of interest could arise between executives and shareholders
- to lead in assessing the performance of the executive team: 'contribution … in reviewing the performance of the board and of the executive.'[17]

The Code also sets out specific tasks:

- constructively challenge and help develop proposals on strategy[18]

[16] Corporate Governance Code SB.3.

[17] Sir Adrian Cadbury, *Corporate Governance and Chairmanship*.

[18] Corporate Governance Code, The Main Principles – Leadership.

- scrutinise the performance of management in meeting agreed goals and objectives
- monitor the reporting of performance
- satisfy themselves on the integrity of financial information
- satisfy themselves that systems of risk management are robust and defensible
- take responsibility for determining appropriate levels of remuneration for executive directors
- have a prime role in appointing and removing executive directors and in succession planning.

To enable them to carry out their role, non-executive directors should:

- benefit from a formal induction process
- meet senior executives, because they may be asked to vote on their appointment to the board
- visit the company's sites
- meet major shareholders
- 'regularly update and refresh their skills and knowledge'[19]

and, as for executive directors, they should be appointed through 'a formal, rigorous and transparent procedure'.[20]

 *Independent non-executive directors should form a majority of the nominations committee and all of the audit and remuneration committees.*

The Code requires non-executive directors to be appointed for a fixed term, subject to re-election but that 'Any term beyond six years....should be subject to particularly vigorous review, and should take into account the need for progressive refreshing of the board.'[21] This leaves some scope for discretion. Cadbury has put forward a balancing view that it may take some years for non-executive directors to maximise their knowledge and be most valuable to a complex company. This implies that a short tenure has the effect of also cutting short the director's usefulness. He proposes that independence of mind and judgement are the necessary qualities required of a non-executive director, which may or may not be captured by the specific rules of a code, such as length of service. The QCA shares this latter view.

[19] ibid. SB.4.
[20] Corporate Governance Code SB.2.
[21] ibid. SB.2.3.

Independent non-executive director

What is an independent non-executive director? The word 'independent' has been added as a reaction against companies appointing 'friends of the chairman' to the board. By having people with family, social or business links as non-executives, companies were able to create an appearance of independence whilst shared experiences and views of the world ensured the board would generally be uncritical of management.

The Code does not strictly define independence but requires the board to identify those it considers to be its independent directors in the annual report and then states that the board should give reasons for this judgement 'notwithstanding the existence of relationships or circumstances that may appear relevant to its determination, including if the director':

- has been an employee of the company or group within the last five years or has had within the last three years
- has received or receives additional remuneration from the company apart from a director's fee, participates in the company's share option or a performance-related pay scheme, or is a member of the company's pension scheme
- has close-family ties with any of the company's advisers, directors or senior employees
- has cross-directorships or has significant links with other directors through involvement in other companies or bodies
- represents a significant shareholder
- has served on the board for more than nine years from the date of their first election.[22]

It has been argued that companies need directors who are '…independent of mind and willing and able to challenge, question and speak up'[23] rather than those who match a tick-box list. It is therefore open to companies to disagree with the list and, for example, to reappoint a director who has served more than nine years, as long as they report and justify the fact. It might be reasonable to argue that an individual has demonstrated independence of mind and judgement that outweighs the risk of having become close to management over time. The QCA guidance emphasises the need for board membership to be 'periodically refreshed' rather than being prescriptive about how to do this.

[22] Corporate Governance Code SB.1.1.

[23] The Higgs Report on the Role of Non-executive Directors, Department for Business Enterprise and Regulatory Reform, 2003, S9.1.

Senior Independent Director

Both the Code and the QCA Guidance require the appointment of a senior independent director ('SID') who can 'provide a sounding board for the chairman and to serve as an intermediary for the other directors where necessary'.[24] 'This aspect of the role is particularly important if, for example, the chairman exerts more than usual influence as a founder, significant shareholder or executive director.'[25]

The SID should also be available to shareholders 'if they have concerns which contact through the normal channels...has failed to resolve.'[26] The Code suggests the SID should attend sufficient meetings with major shareholders to appreciate their issues and concerns. The SID also chairs the non-executives meeting to assess the chairman's performance as part of the board evaluation process.

The QCA guidance adds that, 'where crisis strikes....for example about the future of the chairman, the role will become much more substantial',[27] requiring flexibility to devote extra time in an emergency.

 ### The role of the senior independent director

1 Meet with the other members of the Board without the Chairman present on at least an annual basis in order to evaluate and appraise the performance of the Chairman;

2 Chair the Nominations Committee when considering succession to the role of the Chairman of the Board;

3 Act as a point of contact for shareholders and other stakeholders with concerns which have failed to be resolved or would not be appropriate through the normal channels of the Chairman, Chief Executive and/or Chief Financial Officer; and

4 Act as an alternative point of contact for Executive Directors, if required, in addition to the normal channels of the Chairman and/or the Chief Executive;

5 Meet with the other members of the Board as and when deemed appropriate.[28]

---

[24] Corporate Governance Code SA.4.1.

[25] Quoted Companies Alliance (2010) *Corporate Governance Guidelines for Smaller Quoted Companies*, 31.

[26] Corporate Governance Code SA.4.1.

[27] QCA Guidelines S5.5.

[28] http://www.bg-group.com/AboutBG/Governance/Pages/pgSeniorIndependentAuditor.aspx.

The SID should not generally be someone who is being considered for the role of chairman, since this could compromise their independence. If such a possibility should arise, then it would be best practice that they should step down until they have been ruled out of contention.

Board evaluation

An emerging element of the board's role is to evaluate its own performance, that of its committees and that of its members.[29] This is a requirement of the Code and is promoted by many influential investors, including Calpers, the largest US public pension fund, an activist investor with assets exceeding $210bn.

> *No board can truly perform its function of overseeing a company's strategic direction and monitoring management's success without a system for evaluating itself ... and individual director performance.[30]*

This pursues one of the objectives of good corporate governance, which is to promote board effectiveness. Many large companies use outside consultants to help them with these assessments, albeit the final responsibility lies with the board as a whole. Sir Adrian Cadbury, however, prefers a less structured approach: 'Board effectiveness depends so much on the way in which members of the board work together, that I feel the evaluation process should be carried out collectively, as far as possible.'[31] Informed, as it is, by years of experience the following, derived from his suggestions for a structure for a free-ranging board discussion around a prepared agenda, is a useful starting point:

- **The role of the board** – Is there broad agreement? And is it equally clear to executive management? Do board members feel able to contribute to the strategic goals and direction of the business, to the degree that they feel that they should?
- **Its makeup** – Is the board size and makeup appropriate with appropriate skills and expertise represented and is succession planning adequate? Is the committee structure effective and appropriate?
- **How it works in practice** – Do board members feel they receive the information they need, in the form they need it and in a timely fashion? Does the board have enough time and is that allocated appropriately?

[29] Corporate Governance Code SB.6.

[30] California Public Employees Retirement System, *Global Principles of Accountable Corporate Governance*, s2, http://www.calpers-governance.org/docs-sof/principles/2010-5-2-global-principles-of-accountable-corp-gov.pdf.

[31] Sir Adrian Cadbury, *Corporate Governance and Chairmanship*, 45.

- **Confidence in the company's control systems** – Does this include review and approval of senior appointments? Is there a clear understanding of the control systems and information flows? Does executive management meet its agreed plans and budgets? Are there business surprises and unforeseen outcomes?

The chairman, according to Sir Adrian, should carry out an appraisal discussion with individual directors, although the Code is not prescriptive about how evaluations should be carried out. It does require the whole board evaluation to be externally facilitated at least every three years for FTSE 350 companies; other codes and guidelines also support such reviews and assistance.

The Code also requires the chairman to act as a result of the evaluation by 'recognising the strengths and weaknesses of the board'[32] and adjusting its membership, if necessary. It does not refer to individual development in this context, although the QCA guidance does, particularly if any are felt to be ineffective.

The Code requires the chairman's own performance also to be evaluated annually by a committee of the non-executive directors, chaired by the senior independent director.

Long-term versus short-term focus

Part of the evaluation should relate to board targets and how well they balance short- and long-term objectives.

I was told this by a non-executive director on the board of a company whose business was cyclical and whose results could vary significantly between one year and another. When he joined the board it was a private company, with three institutional shareholders, one of which held more than 50% of the shares, and which decided it wanted the business to become listed, to create a potential exit route. My informant relates that the immediate effect of listing was that executive directors became fixated on the share price, calling the company broker for an explanation for any small changes. They also began to manipulate trading to smooth out their reported results, delaying or bringing forward acquisitions and other transactions, as they felt appropriate. He was very uncomfortable about this change in the way the business was managed but, after a while, far from selling its stake, the biggest shareholder bought the entire business. Interestingly, this led the management to abandon their short-term approach and revert to their previous habit of focusing on long-term value.

[32] Corporate Governance Code BS6.

Briefing Lessons

- **Communication with major shareholders is an important element of setting appropriate objectives.**
- **Pressures exerted by shareholders on management can have unintended consequences.**

The UK government announced a review of corporate governance in 2010, to focus specifically on some of these issues. A comprehensive consultation is to cover areas such as:

- What drives market short-termism?
- Do boards set out their long-term objectives sufficiently clearly?
- How can we encourage shareholders to become more engaged in the company's future?
- Do shareholders have sufficient opportunity to vote on takeover bids?
- Do target boards do enough to consider whether the bid represents value for their shareholders in the long term?
- Does the way in which directors are paid unduly encourage takeover activity?[33]

Unfortunately, fund managers are often themselves judged and remunerated on the basis of short-term results. Inevitably this must affect their focus and increase their pressure on investee companies, in turn, to achieve short-term results. Company boards should resist such pressures: there are also many long-term investors.

One of the changes to the Code in 2010 was the provision for annual re-election of directors of FTSE 350 companies, 'to ensure proper accountability'.[34] A number of organisations, including The Confederation of British Industry, believe that this could accentuate short-termism and lead to individual directors – rather than the board collectively – being targeted at annual general meetings. It also believes that the change may make boards less stable and discourage robust challenges in the boardroom. Of course, 'as with all other provisions of the Code, companies are free to explain rather than comply';[35] but the juxtaposition of this caveat immediately following the change to the Code suggests an awareness that it would be a controversial proposal.

[33] Government News Distribution Service (2010) *Cable Calls for Long-term Focus for Corporate Britain*, 22 September.
[34] Corporate Governance Code, *Preface*, pt. 8.
[35] ibid.

There has been considerable concern about executive remuneration exacerbating a short-term outlook, particularly following the banking crisis that started in 2007.

How to do it:
role of chairman

7

Introduction

The role of the chairman is critical to good governance and to effective perform-ance but the law does not describe the role except as the person who chairs board meetings although, even here, the members present at each meeting can appoint their own chairman.

In the UK business model the chairman is generally a balance to the CEO, albeit working closely with him or her. The Corporate Governance Code requires that the roles of chairman and CEO should not be combined in one person,[1] although previous versions were less prescriptive and merely recommended separation or, in default, a greater representation of independent non-executive directors and formal designation of a senior independent non-executive director. As the Cadbury Committee Code of Best Practice put it in 1992:

> There should be a strong and independent non-executive element on the board, with a recognised senior member.

There are two reasons for separation:

- excessive concentration of power
- the roles are different and incompatible.

For private, owner-managed companies this separation may be inappropriate or too expensive, but it is likely to be pursued as the business grows and takes on outside finance or new shareholders.

A retiring CEO should not be appointed chairman,[2] although the Code recog-nises there may be exceptions and specifies, in that event, that an explanation should be given to shareholders. 'Banks, in particular, have argued that only the incumbent CEO has the knowledge and experience of a large multinational group's operations to fulfil the chairman's role.'[3] Such a progression risks sub-verting the authority of the incoming CEO and continuing the strategies, policies and power of the previous one, without review. Ideally, the role should be an external appointment. The main counter-argument to this best practice is that the role sometimes demands a deep understanding of the industry and of the busi-ness. HSBC, for example, has customarily elevated its CEO to the chairman's role. In 2010, it has departed from this practice and appointed another senior executive to the chairmanship. Whilst the reasons for the subsequent resignation of the CEO are not in the public domain – whether umbrage at being denied the

---

[1] Corporate Governance Code SA.2.1.

[2] ibid. S.A.3.1.

[3] Institute of Directors and Pinsent Masons (2010) *The Director's Handbook: Your Duties, Responsibilities and Liabilities* (3rd edn), Kogan Page.

top spot, whether it was forced or whether the incumbent felt his position would be untenable – it may provide evidence against the practice of promoting a CEO to chairman. A CEO, with a forceful personality, who becomes chairman may dominate a successor and act as if holding both positions, which risks undermining the checks and balances designed to limit the power of any single individual.

The chairman's job is:

- to manage board meetings
- to review board papers
- to ensure an appropriate environment for board meetings
- to manage the board agenda
- to ensure everyone's voice is heard
- to move discussion forward to a resolution
- to oversee the production of complete and accurate board minutes
- to ensure board resolutions are acted upon
- to maintain equality in the boardroom and a spirit of openness.

The chairman too is a board member with a right to express their view. However, it would be good practice to do so at the end of a discussion in order not to pre-empt and suppress debate.

In many companies, the chairman takes overall responsibility for strategy and planning for the future whilst the managing director/CEO is in charge of its implementation and the day-to-day. However, this split of responsibilities is entirely a matter for boards themselves to decide. It is equally common for companies to limit their chairman's role to board and governance matters, particularly if the role is not full time. The chairman should seek to achieve a consensus on each issue, rather than taking formal votes, which may represent a type of failure.

Some companies have the role of deputy chairman, which may be taken by the senior non-executive director. Such a role can be helpful, not just in deputising for the chairman but also to contribute if the chairman and CEO disagree. As an equal to the others, this role can help to resolve differences more easily than another board director. An alternative informal structure is often for the finance director to perform this balancing role, but this tends to be less effective because, in many companies, the financial director reports to the CEO.

Procedures at board meetings

The law largely leaves it up to directors to regulate their own proceedings. However, the Articles of Association of a UK company will set out basic procedures to be followed, such as the notice required of a meeting, how it is to be delivered, the quorum, etc.

The frequency of meetings is left to companies, although their Articles may specify a minimum number. They are usually held at least quarterly and often monthly. In a crisis they may even be daily but,

> Given the specific leadership role of the board, it is important to distinguish board…from management meetings, even in owner-managed enterprises.[4]

Any director may call a directors' meeting by giving notice of it to the directors or by authorising the company secretary (if any) to give such notice, which must be given to each director, but need not be in writing. Common law requires the length of notice given to be reasonable in all the circumstances. Failure to give reasonable notice may invalidate the meeting and any decisions taken at it.

Notice of any directors' meeting must indicate:

- its proposed date and time
- where it is to take place.

If it is anticipated that directors participating in the meeting will not be in the same place:

- how it is proposed that they should communicate with each other during the meeting – dependent on the articles, meetings may be held by telephone or video-conferencing.

Directors can waive their entitlement to notice of a particular meeting, by giving notice to that effect to the company, even after it has taken place provided their waiver is given not more than seven days after the meeting. The directors may appoint any director to chair their meetings; it does not have to be the company chairman. They may terminate the chairman's appointment at any time. Resolutions may be passed at a meeting or (for smaller companies) in writing, signed by all those entitled to attend and vote. The board can delegate authority to sub-committees (see below), and minutes must be kept of board meetings and retained for at least 10 years.

The Institute of Chartered Secretaries and Administrators (ICSA) has produced a code of good boardroom practice,[5] which suggests:

i   The board should establish written procedures that should be part of each director's induction information.

ii   In the conduct of board business:
     a. Each director should receive the same information at the same time
     b. Each director should be given sufficient time to consider this information.

[4] Institute of Directors (2010) *Corporate Governance Guidance and Principles for Unlisted Companies in the UK.*

[5] ICSA (1996) *Good Boardroom Practice: a code for directors.*

iii The board should identify matters requiring their prior approval (see page 103) and lay down procedures to be followed when, exceptionally, a decision is required before its next meeting. Where possible the approval of all directors should be obtained by means of a written resolution. The procedures should balance urgency with the overriding principle that each director should be given as much information as possible and have the opportunity to requisition an emergency meeting of the board to discuss a matter prior to commitment.

iv All material contracts and those not in the ordinary course of business should be referred to the board before agreement.

v The board should define 'material' and 'not in the ordinary course of business' and communicate these to all relevant persons [who might be involved in agreeing such contracts]. Different definitions of 'material' should be agreed for contracts that are 'in' or 'not in the ordinary course of business'.

vi In the event of uncertainty a contract should be referred to the board.

vii Decisions relating to the content of agenda items and their presentation should be taken by the chairman together with the company secretary.

viii The company secretary should be responsible to the chairman for the proper administration of meetings of the company, the board and its committees, should be present at (or represented at) and prepare (or arrange preparation) of minutes of all such meetings.

ix The minutes of the company should record decisions taken and provide sufficient background to those decisions. All papers presented to the meeting should be identified in the minutes and retained for reference. Procedures for the approval and circulation of the minutes should be established.

x Where the articles of association allow the board to delegate any of its powers to a committee the board should give prior approval to its:
a. Membership and quorum
b. Terms of reference
c. The extent of powers delegated to it.

xi The minutes of meetings of such subcommittees (or a written summary) should be circulated to the board prior to its next meeting, when any board member should have the opportunity to ask questions on them.

xii Notwithstanding the absence of a formal agenda item, the chairman should allow any director or the company secretary to raise at any board meeting any matter concerning compliance with this code of practice, with the Memorandum and Articles or with any other regulatory or legal requirement.

Powers reserved by the board

An effective board delegates much of its authority to executive management because a business cannot be run by a formal committee that is not always in session. However, matters that it reserves to itself should be recorded in a formal schedule,[6] not least for the avoidance of doubt.

The schedules below comprise a summarised extract from an ICSA publication.[7] Although specifically drawn up for listed companies (and giving references to the Code), the principles behind the proposals might be considered helpful by a wide range of smaller listed and private companies that are not required to observe the Code. However, smaller companies may wish to retain control over more of the detailed management issues such as recruitment, authorising bank accounts or signing regulatory documents. The tables give the specific authority for the principle and, where blank, indicates a proposal that seems appropriate or which may be considered necessary to fulfil other obligations of the board.

CC   The Corporate Governance Code 2010
CA   Companies Act 2006

Strategy and management

Approval of values, standards and broad policies	
Approval of objectives and strategy	CC A.1
Oversight of operations	
Approval of budgets	
Review of performance	CC A.1

Structure and capital

Changes to capital structure	
Changes to legal structure, tax residence or listing	
Changes to corporate, management or control structure	

[6] Corporate Governance Code SA.1.1

[7] ICSA (2007) *Guidance on Matters Reserved to the Board*.

Financial reporting and controls

Approval of annual report and accounts, half year accounts, interim statements and preliminary announcements

Approval of any significant changes in accounting policy or practice

Ensuring a sound system of internal control and risk management

Approval of dividend policy, declaration of the interim and recommendation of the final dividend

Approval of significant treasury policies

Approving an appropriate statement for inclusion in the annual report

Significant contracts

Major capital project, investments or acquisitions

Contracts not in the normal course of business

Communication

Approval of resolutions and associated documents to be sent to shareholders

Approval of circulars, prospectuses, etc.

Approval of press releases concerning matters dealt with by the board

Board membership and other appointments

Changes to the size, structure or composition of the board

Ensuring succession planning for board and senior management

Appointments to the board

Selection of chairman, chief executive and senior independent director

Appointment/removal of company secretary

Membership and chairmanship of board committees

Appointment, reappointment or removal of external auditor

Remuneration

Determination of remuneration policy for directors, company secretary and senior executives

Determining the remuneration of non-executive directors, subject to shareholder approval

Approval of share incentive plans subject to shareholder approval

Delegated authority

Division of responsibilities between chairman, chief executive and other directors, which should be in writing

CC A.2.1

Approval of terms of reference of board committees

CC A.2.1; B.2.1; C.3.1

Corporate governance

Formal review of board, directors and committee performance	CC A.6
Determining the independence of directors	CC A.3.1
Considering the balance of interest between shareholders, employees, customers and the community	CA 06 s172

Other

Political and charitable donations

Approval of principal advisers

Major changes in the pension scheme

Schedule of matters reserved for board approval

Managing meetings

The work of directors (particularly non-executives), trustees and senior managers of organisations is often concentrated in a few meetings each year. The big challenge is often not with decisions that you disagree with but rather in failure to address the point at all. There are some critical points to remember:

 Every meeting is your meeting.

Always treat every meeting as if it is yours. You may advance your objectives, or fail; you may increase colleagues' respect or not. But it is yours to win or lose.

 Your job is to speak out.

It is immensely difficult to ask difficult questions or to protest. You are a part of a team and to stand out as a disruptive influence, particularly a lone one, is embarrassing. You may jeopardise business relationships or a career by pointing out that the emperor has no clothes or even by asking difficult questions or insisting that a matter is discussed properly. But it is your job. You will be caught up in the repercussions if you were right but did not speak out. There is also the question of self-respect. How will you feel if you don't speak out?

 Is there a clear agenda?

If the purposes of a meeting are not clear then it is immensely difficult to manage. It is also harder to meet those objectives. If a clear agenda is not circulated then make a point of chasing it up **before** the meeting and ensure it does not happen again.

 Have adequate papers been distributed to everyone in advance?

It is quite common for an inner circle of a board to have more complete information than the rest. This is sometimes innocent, with executive directors needing much more detailed information to carry out their roles. However, it may arise from lack of trust or a desire to manipulate. Questions posed by non-executives should expose shortcomings and they must not be tolerated. The non-executive has exactly the same responsibility and legal liability as the other directors, despite their limited time with the company and limited remuneration to reward it. 'I was not told' is a weak excuse that carries the stigma either of incompetence or mendacity.

 Do you need to speak to the chairman beforehand?

Afterwards is probably too late: if you have missed the opportunity to discuss a matter then someone seeking to bury it wins.

 What is not being discussed?

Is there an elephant in the room?

 Control the minutes.

If minutes of a meeting record decisions or disagreements inadequately, then the first step must be to try to have them amended. If this does not produce results, then a board member can circulate a memo to those present to record what was decided. Decisions in meetings can be ignored, subverted or merely reinterpreted through the minutes, so they matter.

Abco is a successful, rapidly growing family business trading in a highly competitive, commoditised market. The three executive directors comprise two brothers and a brother-in-law who share a close relationship. A problem arose because one major customer, accounting for 40% of turnover, began to get increasingly difficult and pushed for their prices to be reduced to a level that would actually be below average cost. A three-year contract was in place, so there was every reason to resist these demands, but the managing director was nervous which worked badly with his likeable personality – he does not like confrontation or ill-feeling in relationships. He is not a good negotiator. Nonetheless, at a board meeting his brother and brother-in-law persuaded him to resist. And, nonetheless, within a few days he had gone back to the customer and backtracked. I make no judgement over the correct course of action. My comment is on process. There were no minutes of that board meeting circulated immediately. If there had been, they might have made the decision stick.

Boards are often at their weakest when discussing strategy. Remember that goals and strategies are often indistinguishable. The board sets goals and agrees strategies designed to meet them. These, however, become the goals for the management below. For example, the goal of increased profit margins is to be met through a strategy of increasing market share – the senior operational management is given the goal of increasing market share which it decides to do though a pricing strategy; implementing a pricing strategy is then handed down to the marketing department as a goal…etc.

A touchstone for governance in this situation is to adopt the SMART acronym. Goals/strategies must be:

Specific	vague generalities really don't mean anything
Measurable	if it can't be measured it can't be managed
Achievable	no point having unattainable objectives
Rational	'market domination' may sound nice but why do it?
Timely	there must be a target time for achievement

A good test for a statement being specific and having any real meaning is to reverse it and see if the result is so ridiculous that it was not worth saying the original phrase. For example, a goal, strategy or published value that talks about trading with integrity is meaningless because who would proclaim they plan to trade without integrity? On the other hand, it would be worth saying that you intend to espouse openness about your business because it is quite possible to argue the opposite, that limiting public disclosure will cut administrative costs and limit possible repercussions.

Constructing a 'boardroom conversation'

There may be disagreement between board members and this can comprise significant differences on material issues, but robust debate of important issues is good: it shows the board is doing its job. It will usually result in a consensus being reached and those who disagree will accept defeat. However, strong personalities may seek to shut down debate without considering the issues adequately.

Professor Bob Garratt comments:

> Walker[8] encourages 'independence of thought' and 'challenge' but says little about practicality. An expectation that an Executive Director would openly challenge their Chief Executive at a board meeting is known in psychology as 'a career threatening opportunity'. Few have been known to accept it.

And this is the rock upon which much of governance theory founders. How can a constructive, free, participative, wide-ranging and challenging boardroom conversation be developed? This is a critical role of chairmanship. The chairman must create the conditions for it. If a chief executive, either through conscious pressure or through sheer force of personality, shuts down open debate, then that individual must be led to a more open style of management. In extreme circumstances, that individual may need to be replaced because, without a properly functioning board, governance is in abeyance.

However, governance models tend to refer solely to the chairman when this is a joint enterprise; the role of the chief executive is also critical. The CEO's job includes selecting and managing the executives. The board nominations committee (see p. 119) will work together with the CEO who will have a significant role in selecting the team he or she will manage. And it is too often forgotten that the CEO is a line manager of those executive directors who are direct reports.[9] Therefore the chairman and CEO must work together to ensure that the executive directors can contribute information and speak freely at board meetings.

The line management of the executive team is also important when considering how the various executive directors must cohere and work as a team.

---

[8] Sir David Walker (2009) *A Review of Corporate Governance in UK Banks and Other Financial Industry Entities*, HM Treasury, 16 July.

[9] Janice Caplan (2010) *The Value of Talent*, Kogan Page.

X was a private high-tech company with a multi-billion pound turnover and institutional shareholders. It had seven executive directors, five non-executive directors and a poisonous internal atmosphere, several individuals who could not stand each other and intense personal rivalries that were continued down the departmental hierarchies. This led to weak cooperation between functional departments and with strategic business units so that the business under-performed.

The chief executive was a capable engineer and strategist, a personable individual who simply had no idea how to manage his team to deal with these frictions and inefficiencies. He would encourage his directors to bring proposals to the executive board but then leave them unsupported and allow the 'ravening pack' to compete for resources and status. The chairman, in particular, and non-executive directors should have played a significant part in resolving the issues of this dysfunctional board, but failed to do so. The department heads had established expert power in their roles and were hard to replace. Although the problems did not result in sudden economic failure or misfeasance, they were entirely of a governance nature based on our definition that it is on the basis of systems, procedures and behaviours that an organisation is managed.

The eventual outcome was that the shareholders replaced almost the entire team, so everyone lost.

Briefing Lessons

The lessons from this example are highlighted by Jack Welch, former CEO of GE. There are four types of managers[10]...

- **Type 1: shares our values; makes the numbers – sky's the limit!**
- **Type 2: shares the values; misses the numbers – typically, another chance, or two.**
- **Type 3: doesn't share the values; doesn't make the numbers – gone.**
- **Type 4 the toughest call: doesn't share the values, but delivers the numbers. The toughest to part with because organisations want to deliver and to let someone go who gets the job done is unnatural. But we have to remove them because they have the power to destroy the open, informal, trust-based culture we need to win today and tomorrow.**

The features that lead to the effective boardroom conversation which is critical to good governance are illustrated in Figure 7.1. It emphasises the leading role of the chairman whose first job is to create an effective partnership with the CEO

[10] Jack Welch, Chairman and CEO of General Electric, in the 2000 annual report.

Figure 7.1 Determinants of the boardroom conversation

who, in turn, leads the executive team. The important word in this sentence is 'team'. A prerequisite of effective governance and an efficient boardroom process is that the chairman is leading a board team and the CEO is leading an executive team: without people working together, the processes falter. The result must be executive directors who are empowered to contribute information and opinions openly at board meetings.

The composition, including diversity, of the board is an essential factor, with the minimum necessity being for them to have necessary skills and be:

- properly Informed
- able to commit sufficient time
- immersed in the business
- in possession of network connections outside the business.

The company secretary is included. Although not legally necessary for private companies and normally not a board member, this role is an important facilitator for the board, working with the chairman to ensure, amongst other things, full and timely provision of information, without which the basis for proper discussion and good decision-making disappears.

The diagram also illustrates the importance of external inputs to enable effective boardroom conversation. External sources include flows of information from within the company and without about markets and technologies and about the whole environment. Tomorrow's Company[11] argues that

> *Effective boards are not insular but, rather have a keen understanding/radar of the external landscape.[12]*

They argue further the importance of widespread business contacts through a network of relationships that contribute powerfully to this. Their research indicates that board members of innovative companies had around 30% more contacts than those in a random sample.[13]

Investors can be an important part of this external influence on companies because the effective boardroom conversation includes a dialogue with shareholders, the importance of which becomes most apparent at times of crisis.

The balanced boardroom

Throughout this book there are difficult balances to hold, whose importance cannot be underestimated. Thus:

- A chairman's relationship with the chief executive is important **but** should not be so close as to exclude challenge or preclude removing the CEO. If the two become a team carrying out a joint enterprise, then the chairman's function is debased.
- Directors should form a coherent team **but** should not be so friendly as to circumscribe the non-executive directors' role of challenging.
- Non-executive directors should be immersed in the business **but** not so much that they become a part of the executive team.
- Independence is important in non-executive directors **but** not to the extent that valuable skills are disbarred.

There is a danger that a compliance mentality may grip a company so that it becomes forgotten that governance codes in the UK operate on a 'comply or explain' basis. Where the balance of utility shifts against the Code, companies must feel free to do what is right and to explain why they are not complying.

[11] Tomorrow's Company describes itself as 'a not-for-profit research and agenda-setting organisation committed to creating a future for business which makes equal sense to staff, shareholders and society.'

[12] Tomorrow's Company and the Department for Business Innovation and Skills (2009) *Tomorrow's Innovation, Risk and Governance*, 54.

[13] Tomorrow's Company and The Department for Business, Innovation and Skills (2009) *Tomorrow's Innovation, Risk and Governance*.

Board committees

Although private companies may have small boards comprising entirely operational management and will probably have no board committees, the ideas that lie behind having these committees in larger companies still carry lessons for the smaller ones. The tasks they perform, and the independence from vested interests that they represent, can be taken into account by decision-makers in the very smallest business. For example, once a business achieves a size where it can afford a non-executive director, that individual might be tasked with an independent review of the statutory accounts, testing assumptions and policies. Similarly, some part of the approach of a nominations committee can be reproduced through considering the tasks and required qualities of a non-executive director and then recruiting to that specification rather than just appointing a friend of the chairman. Finally, senior level remuneration can be informed by the same principles as the remuneration committee.

At the other extreme, large listed companies will have at least the three recommended in the Code:

- audit committee
- nomination committee
- remuneration committee.

There may be others, such as a risk management committee, and perhaps some may be temporary in nature and established to deal with particular issues. A board committee of independent non-executive directors can offer an important independence of view in relation to a takeover bid, whether the company is making or is the target of a bid. In such circumstances, the executive directors may be influenced by the effects on their personal prospects. Conversely, it must be noted that shareholders may sometimes take a short-term view with executives taking the long-term view for the company. This is particularly true with speculators and hedge funds nowadays taking such an active part in UK takeover bids and, generally, seeking quick returns.

The Code requires companies to make the necessary resources available to these committees to carry out their work properly, including appropriate remuneration, information, induction and training, and to pay for outside advice where necessary.

In addition to resources, the Smith Report specifies that executive directors have a common law duty to provide all the directors, and not just committees, with all the information they need to discharge their duties as directors of the company.[14]

What are the tasks of these committees?

[14] Robert Smith (2003) *Audit Committees: Combined Code Guidance*, FRC, S1.9.

Remuneration committee

The Code provides[15] a context to its concern about remuneration stating that 'companies should provide packages to attract, retain and motivate directors'; that these should 'link rewards to corporate and individual performance' and that the performance related element should 'align their interests with those of shareholders'.

Except where stated, the following requirements are extracted from the Code, but best practice should be deduced from other sources too, including the QCA Guidelines[16] (which adopt a more principles based approach) and ABI Guidelines[17] (which generally support the Code but also adopt more stringent requirements).

The Code specifically requires companies to have a remuneration committee comprising at least three independent non-executive directors (two for smaller companies).[18]

The committee's remit should cover setting the remuneration, including pension rights and 'compensation commitments…their directors terms of appointment would entail in the event of early termination'.[19] These responsibilities extend beyond the executive directors and chairman to recommending and monitoring the senior management level below the board.[20]

It should have the resources to obtain expert advice and should have delegated powers so that they do not have to refer back to the full board. This ensures its independence of operational management and ability to act as a restraint on diversion of the company's resources from shareholders to management through high levels of salary, performance-related pay or share options that are not related to performance.

The committee must 'make available its terms of reference, explaining its role and the authority delegated to it by the board'. The phrase 'make available' is clarified to include publication on the company website. The FSA seems to go further in requiring listed companies to provide a 'description of the composition and operation of the issuers' administrative, management and supervisory bodies and their committees'[21] as part of a governance statement included in the annual directors' report.

The Listing Rules[22] require very significant detail on individual director's remuneration in tabular form, including salary and fees, benefits in kind, annual and deferred bonuses, compensation, etc., share options and other long-term incentive schemes. They require disclosure of details of directors' service contracts that exceed one year, 'giving the reason for such notice period'.

[15] Corporate Governance Code DS.1.

[16] QCA (2010) *Corporate Governance: guidelines for smaller quoted companies*.

[17] ABI (2009) *Executive Remuneration – ABI guidelines on policies and practices*.

[18] Corporate Governance Code SD.2.1.

[19] ibid SD.1.4.

[20] ibid SD.2.2.

[21] *FSA Handbook*, Disclosure Rules and Transparency Rules, S7.2.7.

[22] *FSA Handbook*, Listing Rules S9.8.8.

Publication of such detail and use of comparabilities may, however, drive undesirable behaviours amongst those affected, focusing their attention on comparabilities and contributing to the escalating pay differentials discussed below. The authors of the Code were sensitive to this, requiring[23]

- 'performance related elements of… remuneration to be stretching and designed to promote the long-term success of the company'
- use of pay 'comparisons with caution in view of the risk of an upward ratchet of remuneration levels with no corresponding improvement in performance.'
- the committee to be 'sensitive to pay and employment conditions elsewhere in the group…'

The Code and the QCA Guidelines try to focus more on the principles behind setting pay levels.

One of the drivers of corporate governance reform has been a public perception of burgeoning executive pay which was reinforced by the wave of privatisations of nationalised companies in the UK in the 1980s. Directors who had previously been paid at public sector rates suddenly enjoyed dramatic rises in remuneration and benefited enormously from share options on privatisation. The requirement for independence in the setting of executive pay also developed from perceived excesses by executives of public companies and, in particular, from cases where remuneration appeared to soar despite poor company performance. There has also been a perceived reward for failure in very public instances where executives received large payoffs when they were dismissed. A much quoted, recent example is that of Fred Goodwin, chief executive of Royal Bank of Scotland who left with a reported £16m pension fund despite having been held responsible for the disastrous acquisition of ABN Amro, which RBS was deemed, by commentators, to have overpaid for and which left the company dangerously over-extended. As a result, following the financial crisis of 2007, RBS had to be rescued by the UK government.[24]

Goodwin also represents an example of the 'cult of the leader' about which Chris Bones, former Dean of Henley Business School, said:

The 'War for Talent' has fuelled the rise of a phenomenon of the late 20th century: the 'Narcissistic Organisation'. This is one that is led and peopled by individuals who are reinforced in their self-belief every day by systems of reward and promotion that confirm their abilities. These leaders are not just infallible, but they get paid at levels that reinforce their superiority above the rest of us mere mortals.[25]

[23] Corporate Governance Code SD1.

[24] Philip Aldrick, Katherine Griffiths and Mark Kleinman (2009) 'Sir Fred Goodwin's pension topped up to £16m', *The Telegraph*, 26 February.

[25] Chris Bones (2010) 'The Cult of the Leader', http://www.hrmagazine.co.uk/hro/opinion/1018568/the_cult_leader

In many companies, executives are paid as entrepreneurs when, unlike entrepreneurs, they take little personal financial risk. Extreme examples of individuals capturing value in their businesses from shareholders are provided by the high pay levels of dealers in investment banks and, of course, professional footballers. 'Overall, the [English] Football League is now spending 86% of its revenues on total wages ... which is a huge and ultimately unsustainable financial challenge.'[26]

Bones quotes figures to illustrate his argument:

In the UK in 2007 chief executives earned on average 98 times more than the average for all UK full-time workers. Ten years ago the pay differential was 39 times that of the average worker.

And, with some notable exceptions... performance doesn't seem to come into it. Sixty companies at the bottom of the Russell 3000 Index in the US lost $769bn in market value in the five years ending 2004 while their boards paid their top five executives at each firm more than $12bn.

He goes on to say that, 'proponents of the talent myth argued that the driver of this significant increase was the improvement in the underlying performance of the firm'; however, 'research, done again in the US, shows a potentially different explanation .... It...indicates a doubling in the percentage of profits absorbed by the costs of [top executive] compensation...over a period of less than ten years.'[27]

The remuneration committee solution may not be completely successful in restraining excess, containing its own flaws such as comparisons with similar jobs and companies, first recommended in the Greenbury Report and with committees now asked to 'judge where to position their company in relation to other companies'.[28]

As Sir Paul Judge has pointed out, the law of unintended consequences bites and the result turns out to be an inevitable upward spiral. The average comparable figures 'typically show a spread of plus or minus 30%... The remuneration committee then decides where its executive should fit. I have never known a committee prepared to declare that its chief executive is below average... Typically a committee will pitch the salary at around the upper quartile.' Repeating the exercise the next year, with everyone having pitched at the upper quartile 'pure arithmetic means the average must have risen...by about 15% – exactly what it has done since Greenbury was implemented.'[29]

[26] Deloitte LLP, *Annual Review of Football Finance* 2010.

[27] Chris Bones (2010) 'The Cult of the Leader".

[28] Corporate Governance Code SD1.

[29] Sir Paul Judge (2010), *The Sunday Times* 'How we lost grip of top pay', 14 November.

Judge also points out that this continual rise is unsustainable and calls for a return to a multiple that links the top salaries to the lowest within a company.

The Code makes detailed recommendations on performance-related remuneration for executive directors,[30] including:

- The remuneration committee should consider eligibility for bonuses.
- Bonus 'conditions should be relevant, stretching and designed to promote the **long-term success** of the company' (my emphasis).
- Shareholders should approve new long-term incentive schemes and changes in existing ones.
- Normally, shares, options and deferred remuneration should not vest in less than three years. Share options and other long-term incentive schemes should generally be phased, not issued in one block.
- Annual bonuses and benefits should not be pensionable and the remuneration committee should consider the impact of increases close to retirement, i.e the practice of enhancing an individual's pension entitlement on the eve of retirement is discouraged.
- Share options should be issued at a discount only as permitted by listing rules. However, the ABI guidelines come out definitively against any issue at a discount.
- Total rewards should not be excessive and should be subject to challenging performance criteria reflecting the company's objectives.

However, there are few rules on annual as opposed to long-term bonus schemes, with little disclosed apart from the amount paid in the year. Good practice would be to disclose as much as possible about attainment of targets, commensurate with commercial confidentiality.

The Walker Review recommendations extended some of the remuneration issues, albeit applying specifically to financial institutions:

- The remuneration committee should be responsible for establishing overarching remuneration principles across the organisation.
- It should also be responsible for setting remuneration for all 'high-end employees'.
- It should make broad disclosure of remuneration in the annual report for all 'high-end employees' in bands and by business area.
- High-end employees should build up a shareholding.
- Incentive pay should be paid over several years.
- The remuneration committee should, in carrying out its role, consult the risk committee.

[30] Corporate Governance Code, Schedule A.

- If the non-binding AGM vote on the report of the remuneration committee attracts less than 75% of those voting, in favour, then the committee chair should stand for election in the following year.

An important aspect of the remuneration committee's work is transparency. The approach adopted by the UK government is for directors to disclose what they are doing so that shareholders can make informed choices and, for example, vote against directors' remuneration at AGMs. The problem with this approach is that a vote against the remuneration report is only advisory, which may be an embarrassment companies can live with.

 WPP is a large and successful public company founded, in its current form as an advertising and media company, by Sir Martin Sorrell, who remains chief executive. In 1999 a long-term incentive scheme was introduced for its top 20 executives which provided for the company to match an investment they would make in company shares up to fivefold over five years, conditional upon the company performance being in the top quartile for the industry. There was considerable opposition and around 20% of shareholders voted against. The scheme was renewed in 2004 and again in 2009 despite similar votes against and the public opposition of the ABI and PIRC. In the five years to 2007 Sorrell earned over £80m.

WPP has performed well and over 80% of votes were in favour of the scheme. In contrast, 59% voted against Shell's remuneration report in 2009 because targets had been missed yet share bonuses paid. The chairman of the remuneration committee reported that he had exercised discretion to award £3.6m shares to five executives. There is no mechanism for reclaiming these, despite shareholder disapproval.

Briefing Lessons

- **Despite the apparent impunity with which some companies flout best practice on remuneration, the lesson seems to be that attitudes are changing and it may be only a matter of time before directors find themselves voted out of office if they ignore their shareholders' wishes.**

Action over remuneration levels by fund managers representing large shareholders may be constrained by several considerations, such as their own levels of remuneration and their desire for future business from the very investee companies over which they should be exercising stewardship.

The ABI guidelines broadly follow the Code, whilst taking a generally firmer line. Some specific points are:

- 'Annual bonuses should be demonstrably related to performance. Both individual and corporate performance targets are relevant.'[31]

- 'Following payment of the bonus, shareholders will expect to see a full analysis in the Remuneration Report of the extent to which the relevant targets were actually met.'[32]

- 'Pension entitlement on severance can represent a large element of cost... Remuneration committees should identify, review and disclose in their report any arrangements that guarantee pensions with limited or no abatement on severance or early retirement. These would not be regarded as acceptable if included in new contracts. Remuneration committees should demonstrate that the route taken on severance represents the lowest overall cost to the company.'[33]

- 'Shareholders are not supportive of transaction bonuses that reward directors and other executives for effecting transactions irrespective of their future financial consequences.'[34]

The first two points are particularly relevant to the examples above, whilst the third addresses a common abuse and the fourth is relevant to fears of directors taking a short-term approach (p. 96).

Remuneration of non-executive directors should be fixed by the rest of the board, maintaining the principle that directors should not be involved in setting their own remuneration. This should reflect the time, responsibility and commitment necessary for them to perform their role properly.[35] This is a growing problem, with the time commitment necessary having grown considerably over the years. Remuneration should avoid performance-related pay such as share options. The QCA takes a more nuanced view on this, suggesting that 'Payment partly or fully in shares, held during the director's term of office and for a significant period afterwards sends a good signal about the alignment of the director's interests to those of the company's owners.'[36]

Nomination committee

The Code proposes that a nomination committee should lead the process for board appointments. This should help to avoid cronyism, but it should also promote a more professional approach to the role of the non-executive director, in particular.

[31] ABI Guidelines S11(1.2).

[32] ibid. S11(1.5).

[33] ibid. S11(3.9)

[34] ibid. S11(1).

[35] Corporate Governance Code, SD.1.3.

[36] QCA Guidelines, 31.

It proposes that a majority of the committee members should be non-executive and that the company chairman or an independent non-executive should chair it. Sir Adrian Cadbury puts forward a persuasive argument that, as the company chairman bears responsibility for leading the board team, it is appropriate that he or she should be involved, through the committee, in nominating its members. Naturally this does not apply when a successor is sought to the chairman. There is a very similar case to be made for the CEO, who leads the executive team, to be a member of the committee that appoints them.

The Code requires a section of the annual report to describe the work of the committee, including its processes and for an explanation if external advertising or a search consultancy has not been used to select the chairman or a non-executive director.

The key roles of the committee include;

- evaluation of needs followed by drawing up a description of the role and capabilities required to meet it
- succession planning
- periodic refreshing of the board.

Audit committee

The role and workings of audit committees are established in the Corporate Governance Code and further guidance was provided by the Smith Report.[37] Their primary purpose is to provide independent review of operational management's financial reporting rather than to be directly involved themselves. They should, for example, satisfy themselves that there is a proper system and allocation of responsibilities for the day-to-day monitoring of financial controls, but they should not seek to do the monitoring themselves.[38] Their role is:

- to monitor the integrity of the financial statements of the company
- to review the company's internal control and risk management systems
- to monitor and review the effectiveness of the internal audit function
- to make recommendations to the board in relation to the appointment of the external auditor and to approve the remuneration and terms of engagement of the external auditor following appointment by the shareholders in a general meeting
- to monitor and review the external auditor's independence, objectivity and effectiveness
- to develop and implement policy on the engagement of the external auditor to supply non-audit services

[37] Robert Smith (2003) *Audit Committees: Combined Code Guidance*, FRC.
[38] Ibid S1.10.

- to consider management's response to any major internal or external audit recommendations
- to review the company's procedures for handling allegations from whistleblowers.

Where the audit committee's monitoring and review activities reveal cause for concern or scope for improvement, it should make recommendations to the board on action needed to address the issue or to make improvements.[39]

In order to ensure independence it is suggested that:

- The committee should have at least three members, all of whom should be independent non-executive directors (clearly this rule must be adapted for smaller companies).
- The company chairman should not be member.
- Appointment should be by the full board on the recommendation of the nominations committee, if there is one, and in consultation with the audit committee chairman.
- Appointment should be for up to three years, extendable for up to two further terms.
- It is for the committee to decide if non-members should be invited to a particular meeting or agenda item, so that the finance director or chief executive may or may not be present.
- At least annually, it should meet external and internal auditors without management, to discuss issues arising from the audit.
- It must maintain an oversight role and not be drawn into detailed management.

The Smith Report recommends as desirable, but does not specify as a requirement, that at least one member of the audit committee should have '…significant, recent and relevant financial experience, for example as an auditor or finance director of a listed company'.[40] Best practice must surely be that smaller, and private, companies should consider whether they would benefit from such independent financial expertise.

As well as the need for an induction programme for all directors, 'The company should provide an induction programme for new audit committee members. This should include….an overview of the company's business, identifying the main business and financial dynamics and risks.'[41] Membership of the committee imposes an extra burden on members that should be paid for appropriately and should include time for training.

[39] ibid. S2.1.
[40] ibid. S3.17.
[41] ibid. S3.17.

Other recommendations made in the Smith Report are that:

The board should provide written terms of reference …tailored to the particular circumstances of the company.[42]

and

Where there is disagreement between the audit committee and the board, adequate time should be made available for discussion of the issue with a view to resolving the disagreement. Where any such disagreements cannot be resolved, the audit committee should have the right to report the issue to the shareholders as part of the report on its activities in the directors' report.[43]

The Code states that there should be a section in the directors' report covering the role, responsibilities and actions of the audit committee.

Risk committee

The Walker Review recommends that financial institutions should have a chief risk officer and a separate risk committee that reports within the annual report. It should consider taking outside advice so that it can draw on wider risk experience and should specifically report on strategic acquisitions and disposals.

[42] ibid. S4.1.
[43] ibid. S4.4.

How to do it: shareholder rights

8

Introduction

In recent years, concerned governments and thinkers about business have promoted the transparency approach to shareholder democracy. This idea is that if shareholders are given full and timely information about what is going on and the choices affecting a business, then they will be empowered to defend their rights and hold the executive to account.

As discussed previously, this is a powerful idea but suffers two limitations: the shareholder body being far from homogeneous and comprising individuals and groups with very different interests; and the practical impediments that may exist.

Emblematic of a number of shareholder rights is the Companies Act requirement for an annual vote on the remuneration of directors of quoted companies.[1] However, the outcome is not binding on the executive. On the one hand, a lost vote may be embarrassing but, on the other, it really only matters if a shareholder revolt develops into a vote to unseat directors.

Shareholders holding over 5% of the shares in a company can now require it to circulate[2] a written resolution to shareholders in advance of a general meeting, unless the company obtains court agreement that the application is frivolous, vexatious, defamatory or will be ineffective. Following the changes to the law that permit a private company to dispense with an annual general meeting (AGM), 5% of the shareholding body can require directors to call a general meeting if over a year has passed since the last one. Otherwise, a general meeting can be called at the petition of 10% of the voting shares and these shareholders can also require the circulation of a statement from them.

Public companies must still hold an AGM within six months of their financial year-end and 5% of members can require a resolution to be circulated to shareholders and, if they apply before the year-end, this must be without charge to them.[3]

The practical impediments to shareholder rights arise from difficulties in exercising votes in practice. The individual private shareholder who holds shares through a nominee account, perhaps through an ISA[4] or SIPP,[5] will find it difficult to exercise their vote. It is their broker or ISA manager who is on the company share register and who has the voting right, and few of these provide a voting service to their investors.

Institutional investors often also experience similar impediments and may make use of proxy voting services.

---

[1] Companies Act 2006 S439.

[2] ibid. S292.

[3] ibid. S338.

[4] Individual Savings Account.

[5] Self Invested Pension Plan.

Dilution of shareholders

One of the most contentious areas of shareholders rights and corporate governance is that of the dilution of shareholders' interests. Companies issue new shares:

- in payment for acquisitions
- for cash, to raise new funding from investors
- as part of employee share incentive schemes.

In the first case, as long as the acquisition is worth at least as much as the value of the shares issued, then no value has been transferred from the old shareholders to the new ones. However, the percentage stake in the company held by the old shareholders will have been reduced or 'diluted'.

In the second case, shares may be offered to existing shareholders, which means they are not diluted if they take up their allocation. However, if the shares are sold in the market or directly to new investors, through a 'placing', the old shareholders are diluted.

In the third case, whether employees are awarded share options or the shares themselves, the existing shareholders' interest is diluted. This is just another form of remuneration, which has been recognised by a change in accounting standards (IFRS 2[6] and FRS 20[7]) that require companies (except for those using FRSSE[8]) to charge the fair value of options or shares to be issued as an expense to their profit and loss accounts.

The Companies Act 2006 requires[9] any issue of new shares to be offered first to existing shareholders unless their Articles of Association expressly permits this to be over-ridden. There are exceptions, such as employee share schemes and shares issued for non-cash consideration, such as to buy another business. There is normally a resolution tabled at the AGM of a listed company giving directors the right, until the next AGM, to issue shares, up to a limit, without offering them to existing shareholders first. This is called disapplication of pre-emption rights. It enables companies to make small acquisitions without shareholder approval and also to operate employees' share schemes. The ABI and NAPF, on behalf of investors, provide guidelines as to what they will find acceptable. Institutional investors can get very exercised about over-generous schemes and the ABI guidelines set a maximum of 10% of the share capital to be available for them in any 10-year period, from which 5% may be for executive schemes.[10]

[6] International Financial Reporting Standard 2: share-based payment, International Accounting Standards Board.

[7] Financial Reporting Standard 20: share-based payment, Accounting Standards Board.

[8] Financial Reporting Standard for Smaller Entities, Accounting Standards Board.

[9] Companies Act 2006 S561.

[10] ABI (2009) *Executive Renumeration – ABI guidelines on policies and practices*, S8.1, 8.2.

Shares earmarked for employees may be held in Employee Share Ownership Trusts, and the ABI also requires them to fall within the dilution guidelines and expresses opposition to companies placing more shares into these than are required to meet outstanding liabilities. They also insist that unvested shares are not voted in general meetings, since otherwise a scheme may be used to defend management against market disciplines.

Communication with shareholders

Transparency may be an important route to shareholder rights, but what motivates companies to 'buy-in' to it? There are three reasons of self-interest:

- compliance
- reputation management
- shareholder power.

If there are requirements of law or stock exchange regulation then, clearly, companies will be inclined to comply. However, enforcement is not strong, it being up to the FSA to spot infractions and bring proceedings to force compliance.

The desire of companies to manage their reputation provides powerful positive reinforcement because it becomes part of their total brand and therefore links in with their image with customers, employees and business partners.

Finally, shareholders come into their own at times when they are needed. This means that when a company needs to raise funds or is actually, or potentially, subject to a takeover bid, the directors will be particularly keen to woo their shareholders. A good management team will not wait for a crisis to occur and will be keen to maintain good relationships with shareholders through demonstrating good governance and through excellent shareholder communications.

William Morrison founded the eponymous supermarket chain in 1899 and it became a significant regional chain under his son, chairman and chief executive, Sir Ken Morrison, becoming a member of the FTSE 100 index.

Whilst complying with legal and listing requirements, the company set its face against having non-executive directors, resulting in pressure from shareholder groups to vote against the annual report and accounts.[11]

Things only began to change after Morrisons' acquisition of Safeway in 2003 for £2.9bn. Sir Ken needed to raise money for the bid and institutions insisted he appoint at least two non-executive directors. The acquisition did not go well. There were problems with the different image and market positioning of the firms, with logistics and accounting systems. The year after the deal, profits fell

[11] Adriana Zea and Lois Fettis (2002) 'Morrisons say no to no-execs', *AccountancyAge*, 18 July.

and plummeted into losses the year after that. Shareholder criticism and a weak share price led to gradual change: the board acquired a majority of independent non-executive directors, the roles of chairman and CEO were split and board committees established.

Principles, published by the Pre-Emption Group,[12] advises listed companies that investors will take a more positive attitude to share issues that bypass existing shareholders in circumstances that include:

- the strength of the business case
- the stewardship and governance of the company.

 Briefing Lesson

- **Investors should not be taken for granted until their votes or their cash are suddenly needed – it may be too late then.**

The watchword nowadays is 'engagement' between companies and investors. Companies communicate with their shareholders through:

- annual and interim report and accounts
- market announcements of potentially price-sensitive information (on an ad hoc basis)
- the annual general meeting
- meetings with major shareholders
- the company website.

Best practice is to use these media to go beyond regulatory requirements. The largest companies also communicate by meeting journalists from the national press and many businesses will meet with trade press specific to their industry in order to communicate more effectively with business partners. Many, particularly public companies, employ public relations consultants to assist these processes.

Minority shareholders

The rights of minority shareholders are an important aspect of corporate govern-ance and an extreme example of shareholders not being a homogeneous group. The reality is that they may often be in a weak position: unable to block special

---

[12] Pre-Emption Group (2008) *Disapplying Pre-Emption Rights: A Statement of Principles*.

resolutions that can result in dilution of their shareholding or changes to their rights (unless there are provisions in the Articles that give them a veto); unable to force the company to pay dividends; and unable to influence policy. The governance issue is 'what is proper, in all the circumstances?'

There is protection, but it may be an expensive route to follow; the Companies Act[13] allows for application to the court for an order on the ground that the company's affairs are being or have been conducted in a manner that is unfairly prejudicial to the interests of its members or 'of some part' of them. It relates to cases such as directors misapplying assets for their own benefit or using funds to inflate salaries beyond what is reasonable rather than pay dividends. The court has complete discretion and may order the majority to buy-out the minority at a fair price, or to compensate the company. Alternative routes are to apply to the courts:

- to wind up the company on 'fair and equitable grounds'[14]
- to stop actions that are outside the powers of the directors (ultra vires)
- for directors to compensate the company for breach of their duties – this is a derivative claim, where the controlling directors are, say, diverting business to another company control.

Minority shareholders in listed companies may have more rights since they are covered by the FSA's Listing Rules. However, companies can delist if they can obtain a 75% vote in favour so a minority of less than 25% does not have this protection.

Disclosure requirements

Much of the disclosure requirement for companies is enshrined in company law and listing requirements that are backed by law, rather than in voluntary codes. This corpus of law has grown significantly in breadth and detail over the past 30 years. One of the key pieces of legislation for larger companies is The Large and Medium-sized Companies and Groups (Accounts and Reports) Regulations 2008, which prescribes detailed disclosures in the annual report. Whilst there is clearly a balance to be struck, there is a risk that this prescriptive regime gives company boards a target to avoid if they want to, and many company reports that appear to comply fail to address significant shareholder interests.

The QCA takes a different approach in emphasising the positive role and opportunities of shareholder communication and urges an active engagement:

[13] Companies Act 2006 S994.
[14] Insolvency Act 1986 S122(1)(g).

...transparency and trust between boards and shareholders are of the utmost importance...these factors will both promote the success of the company and reduce the demand for greater regulation....Constructive and active engagement will build trust between boards and shareholders. Corporate governance reporting is as much about building trust as it is about describing the mechanics of...processes. Shareholders should seek to understand and test such reporting so that they can make informed decisions about the quality of a company's corporate governance.[15]

Without seeking to reproduce the Companies Act in full, the key disclosure requirements through shareholder reports are as follows.

Annual report

- A statement of how the board operates including a high-level statement of which types of decisions are to be taken by the board and which delegated.
- Identification of director's roles including on sub-committees.
- Names of independent non-executive directors, with reasons they are considered independent, where necessary.

There is an extensive legal requirement to declare directors' remuneration in the annual report. In addition, the Code, whilst encouraging a limited release of executive directors to take non-executive roles on other boards, requires disclosure of any payments due and whether the individual keeps them.[16]

Business review

The Companies Act 2006 divides companies into three groups: small, medium and others:

*A company is small if it satisfies two out of three conditions; turnover below £5.6m; balance sheet total below £2.8m; employees below 50 **and** is not a public company or engaged in financial services business.*[17]

A company is medium-sized if it satisfies two out of three conditions; turnover below £22.8m; balance sheet total below £11.4m; employees below 250.[18]

Companies falling within the definition of small are not required to have their accounts audited, but many do because it is a requirement of shareholders or

[15] QCA (2010) *Corporate Governance Guidelines for Smaller Quoted Companies*, 4.
[16] Corporate Governance Code SD.1.2.
[17] Companies Act 2006. Ss382–383.
[18] ibid. S465.

financiers or because they believe the accounts will carry more weight (such as if the owners seek to sell the business).

Unless subject to the small companies' regime, the directors' report must contain a business review[19] that will help members to assess how directors have performed their duty to promote the success of the company. Even small companies, however, may conclude that much of this information would be useful to shareholders and financiers and provide it voluntarily. Inter alia the review must contain:

- 'a fair review of the company's business, and
- a description of the principal risks and uncertainties facing the company'.

It should be 'a balanced and comprehensive analysis of:

- the development and performance of the company's business during the financial year, and
- the position of the company's business at the end of that year, consistent with the size and complexity of the business.'

This last phrase is important because the legislators recognised the differences between large and small businesses.

'In the case of a quoted company, the business review must, **to the extent necessary for an understanding of the development, performance or position of the business** [my emphasis], include:

- the main trends and factors likely to affect the future development, performance or position of the business during the financial year, and
- information about:
  - environmental matters (including the impact of the company's business on the environment
  - the company's employees, and
  - social and community issues
- Information about 'persons with whom the company has contractual or other arrangements which are essential to the business of the company'.[20]

This last point is less onerous than it seems at first sight. It is meant to identify critical business relationships (a 'person' can be a company), if any, that shareholders need to know about to make informed judgments. It is not asking for unreasonable detail. There is also a caveat that disclosure is not required if it would 'in the opinion of the directors be seriously prejudicial to that person and contrary to the public interest'.

[19] ibid. S417 (1)–(11).
[20] ibid. S417.5.c.

The 'social responsibility' disclosures could also be avoided if not 'necessary for an understanding…' etc.

'The review must, **to the extent necessary for an understanding of the development, performance or position of the business** [my emphasis], include:

- analysis using financial key performance indicators, and
- **where appropriate** (my emphasis), analysis using other key performance indicators, including information relating to environmental and employee matters'.[21]

Companies defined as medium-sized need not comply with the non-financial elements of this information.

The review of company law in the early 2000s examined three proposals to improve corporate governance:

- requirement for an operating and financial review ('OFR') in the report and accounts
- a statement of directors' duties
- more effective machinery for shareholders to exercise effective (and responsible) control.

In the event, the OFR, introduced in 2005, was then downgraded to the business review that is meant to be 'less prescriptive' and 'more flexible', with the Companies Act 2006 not actually specifying so much detail. However, various bodies (such as the ABI) have sought to bring OFR into the Code, and the Accounting Standards Board has made it into a voluntary statement of best practice. The upshot may be that listed companies, at least, report on a basis that will be little different from the original OFR. In addition, it is likely that the requirement, or something like it will be reintroduced (see p. 24). Significant differences between the OFR and the Review are:

- While both reports required a balanced and comprehensive review, the OFR required an analysis of the wider trends affecting the business whereas the business review covers only performance and development through the year.
- The OFR required commentary on business objectives, capital structure and resources whereas the only essential element of the business review is a summary of principal risks and uncertainties.
- The business review specifies financial and non-financial key performance indicators (including, where appropriate, environmental and employee matters) but not social and community issues, receipts and returns to shareholders and persons with whom the company has key relationships.

[21] ibid. S417.6.

- There is no exemption in the business review for commercially sensitive information, unlike the OFR, but the lesser requirements of the former mean that this difference is not significant.
- The Companies Act 2006 has a non-mandatory requirement for directors to present an enhanced business review that includes forward-looking performance indicators, comment on social, community and employee issues, and environmental matters, whereas the OFR would have made this compulsory.
- The OFR would have had to be audited.
- The OFR should assist the members of the company to assess the strategies adopted by it and to evaluate the potential for them to succeed.

The main risks associated with this enhanced reporting are that:

- The disclosures, particularly on environmental and community matters, turn out to be uncorrelated with performance.
- Systems and procedures are disclosed, but behaviours are at odds with them.

Note some of the highlighted adjectives that are included in the legislation.

As previously mentioned, the Companies Act specifies that the review must be **fair** and include an assessment of the main risks and uncertainties facing the company. It must also be a **balanced** and **comprehensive** analysis.

These information requirements can, however, be omitted if they are not necessary to support the main obligation, but what information is not supplied must be stated.

There may be a natural tendency for boards to try to limit disclosure, both in order to avoid publishing price-sensitive information and also to avoid outside pressure on them over the details of their management. Only time will tell how widely words such as 'fair', 'balanced' and 'comprehensive' will be interpreted and how breaches of the obligations will be dealt with.

Each director, regardless of whether they are non-executive or a specialist in a particular area, is required to take the steps necessary to be aware of relevant audit information, exercising reasonable care skill and diligence, and to make sure the auditors are aware of that information. Failure to do this, either knowingly or through reckless failure of duty, can be punishable by up to two years' imprisonment or/and a fine.

A director may be personally liable for losses suffered, but only to the company and not to shareholders or any third party.[22] However, there may be a derivative claim by a shareholder who brings it on behalf of the company and must get the court's permission to do so.[23]

The intention of greater disclosure (Code requirements) is to empower shareholders to be informed to apply pressure and be involved in decision-making.

[22] Companies Act 2006 S463.
[23] ibid. Ss260–264.

Price-sensitive information[24]

A listed company must release price-sensitive information (inside information) through an approved Regulatory Information Service as soon as possible to prevent a false market but may delay if:

- that will not mislead the public
- any person receiving the information owes the company a duty of confidentiality
- the company can ensure confidentiality.

There is no obligation to disclose information on negotiations prematurely if that might affect their outcome, but announcement of financial difficulties cannot be delayed just because that would prejudice a negotiating position. In such circumstances, the fact of the difficulties must be announced, albeit the details of negotiations underway to address them may be withheld.

Listed companies must restrict inside information internally on a 'need to know' basis and must be prepared with a 'holding statement' in the event that a breach of a duty of confidentiality leads to rumours.

Failure to make or delay in announcements or in the relevant detail has led to substantial fines for listed companies and their directors under the FSA's Disclosure and Transparency Rules. AIM and PLUS companies would be penalised under their respective listing rules or under the market abuse regime.[25]

[24] FSA Listing Rules S2.5.
[25] Financial Services and Markets Act 2000, S118.

How to do it: role of markets

9

Introduction

One of the main objectives of good corporate governance is to protect investors and to ensure that markets operate properly.

> *Business ethics matters to society because distrust is a real barrier to the flow of information and of trade. Confidence is important as a basis of business, and so society as a whole is impoverished if business standards slide. If that slide results in increased regulation, then that is a costly, and often inefficient, alternative.*[1]

But equally, investors are expected to ensure that companies are governed properly. To this end, the Companies Act and Corporate Governance Code are concerned with the provision of information to investors to enable them to exert informed control. This is the philosophy behind the UK's 'comply or explain' approach which is founded upon a belief that if company directors believe that it is more efficient not to comply with a provision of the Code and they explain this, then investors can and will decide whether they agree.

This concept is based on rather more complex issues than may be obvious at first sight. UK Office for National Statistics survey data suggests that around 40% of UK shares are held by overseas investors, just 10% by individuals and the rest, largely, by institutional investors.[2]

Nearly a quarter of companies listed on the London Stock Exchange are incorporated overseas and many have dual listings on other stock markets. The role of institutional shareholders is therefore complicated. Of course, just because they are located overseas does not mean that investors are not interested in good corporate governance and stewardship, but this highlights the international nature of the issue.

An important problem with investors taking an active interest in governance is the cost of resources this can entail. For many, it is preferable to sell their shares if they are unhappy. Newspaper reports that investors were unhappy with governance issues at ENRC also stated that a major institution had sold most of its shares in protest (see p. 140). Whilst this may have registered a protest, it also removed their previous influence. Investors who operate index funds are not set up to pick and choose or to devote resources to managing individual investments while, at the other extreme, hedge funds often get actively involved in their investments but on specific business issues aimed at increasing value and they are often very short-term investors.

[1] Sir Adrian Cadbury (2002) 'Business dilemmas: ethical decision making in business', in Christopher Megane and Simon Robinson, *Case Histories in Business Ethics*, Routledge.

[2] Office for National Statistics, Share Ownership Bulletin 2008. This data is based on surveys of the share registers of the largest UK listed companies, which account for 85% of stock-market value. We therefore do not know whether this holds also for smaller companies.

The terms 'shareholder' or 'investor' are not so simple: there is the asset owner and also the fund manager who may invest on their behalf; there are also practices such as lending shares, pooled investments and investing in share derivatives. In these circumstances, who should be exerting influence on directors of an investee company?

The UK's Financial Reporting Council published a Stewardship Code in 2010[3] whilst also considering making it a regulatory requirement for UK authorised investment firms to report their compliance with it on a 'comply or explain' basis. This code establishes seven principles for institutional investors to:

- publicly disclose their policy on how they will discharge their stewardship responsibilities
- have a robust policy on managing conflicts of interest in relation to stewardship and this policy should be publicly disclosed
- monitor their investee companies
- establish clear guidelines on when and how they will escalate their activities as a method of protecting and enhancing shareholder value
- be willing to act collectively with other investors as appropriate
- have a clear policy on voting and disclosure of voting activity
- report periodically on their stewardship.[4]

Of these, the detail given for principle three is particularly interesting, 'to satisfy themselves, to the extent possible, that the investee company's board and committee structure are effective and that independent directors provide adequate oversight'. It advocates doing this through meeting the chairman or other board members, if appropriate. It ties this Stewardship Code to the UK Corporate Governance Code by requiring investors to 'consider carefully explanations given for departure from the [Code]' and to 'be prepared to enter a dialogue if they do not accept the company's position'.[5]

There is also an important caveat to this role in that 'institutional investors may not wish to be made insiders' and 'will expect that investee companies and their advisers will ensure that information that could affect their ability to deal in the shares of the company concerned is not conveyed to them without their agreement'.[6]

Individuals find it difficult to hold executives to account through voting at general meetings because their holdings are small. On the other hand, they are able to apply significant pressure through forming campaigning groups which focus on creating publicity to influence institutional investors or which is aimed directly

---

[3] FRC (2010) *UK Stewardship Code*.

[4] ibid. 6.

[5] ibid. 6.

[6] ibid. 6.

at companies' customers. These campaigns are generally related to corporate social responsibility issues ranging from animal rights to human rights and environmental matters.

There is also a stewardship agenda for private companies, usually through investment by private equity and venture capital investors. Members of the British Venture Capital Association still invested £3bn in 834 UK companies in 2009 (2007: £12bn)[7], making them a potentially important influence on governance. Clearly, their approach is primarily to safeguard their investments by ensuring that management teams act properly and effectively and that information flows allow investors to understand and assess progress in the business. They often nominate non-executive directors, which raises a governance issue, since under UK company law a director's responsibility is to the company and not to whoever nominated them. For example, suppose an investor wanted an early sale to realise value but that was not in the interests of the company (and presumably not in the long-term interests of other investors), then a director nominated by that investor would be acting unlawfully in representing its interests. Presumably an action could be brought against the director in the name of the company.

Activist shareholders and fund managers

There has been a long-standing City tradition of investors making discreet approaches to company management to express concerns they may have. In times past when the City shared many characteristics of a club, with reputation being critical, such a system offered some constraints on bad behaviour. With the opening up of markets, an individual who is snubbed by one prospective adviser may simply find another. For example, Robert Maxwell, criticised by a government inspector as 'unfit to run a public company' had re-emerged some years later as chairman of a public company. Surely the last word on this is Myners's stricture 'Merely meeting senior management and expressing polite reservations about strategy is not sufficient if it is not effective.'[8]

Activist fund management

There are several different types of activist fund management:

- Ethical investment funds
- Active engagement funds
- Occasionally active
- Activism as a strategy.

[7] BVCA (2009) *Private Equity and Venture Capital Report on Investment Activity*.

[8] Paul Myners (2001) *Myners Review of Institutional Investment: Final Report*, HM Treasury.

Ethical investment funds

Some investment funds specialise in socially responsible investing, which in 2001 was estimated to account for 5% of all funds invested in the UK.[9]

Active engagement funds

These are funds that seek active engagement with their investee companies as part of their investment philosophy. Large investors such as Calpers[10] in the USA, Lens and Hermes[11] in the UK publish their own governance codes that describe additional steps they expect their investee companies to take.

Occasionally active

Many investing institutions will take an active stance on occasions by expressing concerns to the board, by publicising their concerns to the media, by voting against board resolutions or by putting forward their own resolutions. How easy it is for institutions to combine to be effective is hard to ascertain.

In October 2010 Eurasian National Resources Corporation (ENRC) caused a furore when it bought mineral exploration rights in the Democratic Republic of Congo (DRC). These had been repossessed by the DRC government in 2009 from First Quantum, another mining company listed in London: an act which was subject to international legal action. The confiscated rights had then been sold to an investor for $20m, who promptly sold them on to ENRC for $175m. Transparency International's Corruption Perception Index for 2009 placed the Democratic Republic of Congo at joint 162nd in the world out of 180 countries.

Two big City institutions reportedly met with ENRC representatives to express concern whilst a third reportedly sold most of its holdings in protest.[12] The Sunday Times *also reported that ENRC's brokers had come under investor pressure to reconsider their position, and that 'The deal caused a split at ENRC. Sir Paul Judge, a [non-executive] board director, voted against it while three others abstained'. However, Sir Richard Sykes, who is senior independent director and a former chairman of Glaxo Smith Kline, defended the transaction, arguing that First Quantum's dispute is with the DRC government and not with ENRC and that political risk is part and parcel of the mining industry.*

[9] European Commission (2001) *Promoting a European Framework for Corporate Social Responsibility*, COM (2001) 366 final.

[10] The California Public Employees Retirement System is the largest US public pension fund with assets exceeding $210bn.

[11] Hermes, a leader amongst activist investors in the UK, is a wholly owned subsidiary of the BT pension scheme and has over £60bn under management.

[12] Danny Fortson (2010) 'City firms join Congo protest', *The Sunday Times*, 3 October; 'City fury at Sykes Congo deal', *The Sunday Times*, 19 September.

There is an ethical argument that ENRC is in receipt of stolen property, but there is a robust counter-argument that the government seizure was legal, for cause and untainted by corruption.

 Briefing Lessons

- **Institutional investors have expressed their views forcibly, both directly and, apparently, through press briefings.**
- **When the furore dies down, it looks likely that serious issues will be decided by international courts rather than by investors.**
- **There is clear evidence of a robust boardroom debate, which may be indicative of non-executive directors doing their job properly.**

Amongst the activist shareholders a number promote ethical investment, one element of which is honesty. It is often averred that trust, honesty and integrity are critical for business, but is this necessarily true, and if it is true, which parties to what sort of deal need to trust each other? Newspaper reports and the publications of Transparency International indicate that India, China and Russia are amongst the more corrupt countries with, in the case of China and Russia, a fairly patchy rule of law. Yet two of the three are displaying rapid economic growth.

Activism as a strategy

A final group of investors take stakes in underperforming companies and then campaign aggressively to pressure the board to change its strategy or business practices. Their goal is to achieve a higher share price as a result of the reforms they seek, often followed by a sale of their stake for a substantial profit.

This last category of active investor may exemplify a short-term approach but may also reinvigorate underperforming companies. Some large funds will take a substantial stake in their target company which will exert significant pressure on its own; others may only have a small percentage of the votes but, through persuading other investors, publicity, speaking at general meetings, direct contact with the company directors, etc. will achieve change.

 In late 2010 Laxey Partners, an avowedly short-term investor, based in the Isle of Man, took a 1.5% stake in Alliance Trust, a £2.4bn investment trust based in Dundee. It used this as a platform to agitate for a reduction in the quoted company's 16% discount to its underlying asset value (compared to a 10% norm in the sector) through the company buying back its own shares. It commissioned an independent report, at a cost of £50,000, used publicity to gain support from other investors and instigated a shareholder resolution to be voted on at the company's 2011 AGM.

Making votes count

For shareholders to hold management to account or to encourage a change of course, the key question is how effective the individual shareholder's vote can be. As described above, change can be instituted by persuading other shareholders so that the small individual vote is leveraged through a campaign. However, there is another aspect of this. Can pension funds, for example, vote shares that they hold through fund managers or through nominee accounts? In the past, fund managers would often fail to vote the shares they held on behalf of others but, increasingly, they offer effective mechanisms to allow the beneficial holder's views to be heard. This can result in one fund manager, who has invested on behalf of several pension or insurance funds, voting different blocs of shares in different ways. It has led to the growth of proxy advisory companies and to active investors pursuing increasingly complex strategies to reach decision-makers and to make their votes count.

Similar questions about the exercise of votes can apply to investors in unit or investment trusts or other investment vehicles. Normally the individual stake is too small to have influence and the fund manager will decide whether or how to exercise votes. However, it is always possible to write to the fund manager and request them to take a particular stance.

Another category of the disenfranchised is the company's own employees, who may hold shares through various share ownership schemes. Whilst these are normally automatically voted in favour of incumbent management, it may not be impossible to persuade trustees that the balance of their responsibilities should lead them elsewhere.

Insider dealing

What is insider dealing and why does it matter? It is a particular case of a conflict of interest that may damage the interests of shareholders but certainly defrauds people the 'insider' buys from or sells to. It is a fraud because the insider makes use of information that is not publicly available to gain a financial advantage. Unfortunately, it has often been viewed with equanimity amongst brokers as being perfectly reasonable behaviour, and insider dealing has only been a criminal offence in the UK since 1980.[13]

There are three ways in which an individual who has inside information can commit a criminal offence:[14]

[13] 'Insider dealing in the city', speech by Margaret Cole, Director of Enforcement, FSA, London School of Economics, http://www.fsa.gov.uk/pages/Library/Communication/Speeches/2007/0317_mc.shtml.

[14] Criminal Justice Act 1993 S52.

- Dealing in securities themselves
- Encouraging another person to deal in securities
- Disclosing the inside information.

There are defences, such as that the information was already in the public domain or that the individual would have acted in the same way even without the inside information.[15]

The FSA has indicated its determination to prosecute those guilty of insider trading and has secured a number of convictions during 2010 that have resulted in jail sentences and confiscation orders.

The Code of Market Conduct[16] defines an 'insider' as any person who has inside information as a result of:

- membership of the administrative, management or supervisory body of an issuer of qualifying investments
- holding capital of an issuer of prescribed investments
- having access to the information through their employment, profession or duties
- criminal activities or which they have obtained by other means, e.g. a tip-off from a friend, and which they know, or could be reasonably expected to know, is inside information.

Moreover, it could be a relation or associate of an insider or someone to whom inside information is disclosed. The law applies to anyone who has inside information just by virtue of having it and so the rules should be publicised within any listed company. It includes major investors if they are 'made insiders' through receiving information, for example, during a company briefing, or an indiscreet disclosure by a director of the company.

There are three possible offences:

- criminal offence
- breach of Listing Rules and the Model Code
- a civil offence of market abuse.

Inside information

This is information that:

---

[15] The FSA and insider dealing, http://www.9bedfordrow.co.uk/87/records/1/The%20FSA%20and%20Insider%20Dealing.pdf.

[16] FSA (2001) *Code of Market Conduct*.

- relates to particular securities
- is specific or precise
- has not been made public
- if it were made public, would be likely to have a significant effect on the price of any securities.[17]

Using insider information for trading shares has not always been illegal and, even after it was made so, has often been regarded as fair by many market traders.

The civil offence, as defined in the FSMA,[18] can be any of seven types of behaviour:

1 **Insider dealing** – when an insider deals, or tries to deal, on the basis of inside information.
2 **Improper disclosure** – where an insider improperly discloses inside information to another person.
3 **Misuse of information** – behaviour based on information that is not generally available but would affect an investor's decision about the terms on which to deal.
4 **Manipulating transactions** – trading, or placing orders to trade, that gives a false or misleading impression of the supply of, or demand for, one or more investments, raising the price of the investment to an abnormal or artificial level.
5 **Manipulating devices** – trading, or placing orders to trade, which employs fictitious devices or any other form of deception or contrivance.
6 **Dissemination** – giving out information that conveys a false or misleading impression about an investment or the issuer of an investment where the person doing this knows the information to be false or misleading.
7 **Distortion and misleading behaviour** – behaviour that gives a false or misleading impression of either the supply of, or demand for, an investment; or behaviour that otherwise distorts the market in an investment.

What penalties can be imposed for market abuse? The criminal offences of making misleading statements or engaging in a course of misleading conduct and insider dealing are punishable by a maximum of seven years' imprisonment or an unlimited fine. The civil disciplinary regime allows for a wider range of penalties to be imposed. The FSA may impose a financial penalty or make a public statement about the behaviour and can apply for an injunction restraining market abuse or an order for restitution.

[17] Criminal Justice Act 1993 S56.
[18] Financial Services and Markets Act 2000 S118.

Market manipulation

An issue closely related to insider dealing is that of market manipulation, which is a practice almost as old as share trading itself. Indeed, practitioners would feel themselves ill-used to be disciplined for what they felt was a normal part of business.

 Perhaps the earliest case was that of Scott v Brown Doering McNab & Co *1892 which hinged on brokers creating a false market in a new share issue to excite interest and attract buyers. Over time, the broker would withdraw their market support and hope that improved trading would maintain the share price or, having achieved the purpose of the share issue, allow it to fall to its natural level. The dispute ended in court and 'one of the defendants declared, "you only have to ask anyone about new companies if it [that is, creating a false premium] is not a necessity."'*

The judge, however, took a remarkably different view, and what he said was:

I do say that if persons, for their own purposes of speculation, create an artificial price in the market by transactions which are not real, but are made at a nominal premium merely for the purpose of inducing the public to take shares, they are guilty of as gross a fraud as has ever been committed.[19]

The Guinness case, when that company acquired Distillers in (1987) was similar, the bidder's merchant bank having organised purchases of its shares by selected investors who would be indemnified against any losses and paid for their trouble, in an effort to keep the share price up. The element of fraud is that Distillers shareholders were induced to accept Guinness shares that were worth less than they thought from the quoted share price. Several of those involved spent time in prison.

Takeovers

The Takeover Panel has statutory authority, under the Companies Act 2006, to make rules and regulations in respect of takeovers and mergers of listed companies, to demand information and to impose penalties for non-compliance. The requirements of The Takeover Code that relate to governance issues are summarised below, but these would also be good practice for unlisted companies that are involved in acquisitions.

It is common for boards to delegate authority, to deal with making or defending a bid, to selected directors or to a committee. However, the Takeover Code requires that board members must be provided promptly with documents and must be 'kept up to date with events and with actions taken'.[20]

[19] Sir Adrian Cadbury in Megone and Robinson, op. cit.
[20] The Panel on Takeovers and Mergers (2009) *The Takeover Code*.

The Code states six broad principles, of which the first two have significance for corporate governance:

- All holders of the securities of an offeree company of the same class must be afforded equivalent treatment.
- The holders of the securities of an offeree company must have sufficient time and information to enable them to reach a properly informed decision.[21]

It requires that the boards of the offeree and offeror companies 'must obtain competent independent advice on any offer and the substance of such advice must be made known to its shareholders'. There must be equality of information to all shareholders, and incentives offered to the management of an offeree company by the offeror must be disclosed.

Directors are required to take responsibility for documents issued during public bids and the guidance notes to the Takeover Code draw attention to sections of the Financial Services and Markets Act that make issuing false and misleading statement unlawful.[22] A reckless statement would be caught under these provisions.

There are special rules for management buyouts, where the independent non-executive directors must, on request, be furnished with the same information supplied to financiers. Directors involved in the buyout, who would therefore have a conflict of interest, would not then be party to the circular that must be sent to shareholders expressing the views of the board on an offer. In the event of a split in the board, the views of the minority should also be circulated.

[21] ibid. General Principles.
[22] Financial Services and Markets Act S397.

How to manage corporate governance

10

Introduction

The relationship between chairman and chief executive is critical and the chairman's role is pivotal. In the first place, given that the law largely leaves it to companies to organise themselves, the two individuals must agree which of them does what and where their roles may overlap. This should usually be agreed whenever a new chairman or chief executive joins, but roles and individuals do develop and so these matters should be reviewed from time to time. The Code suggests that the division of responsibilities should be 'clearly established, set out in writing and agreed by the board'.[1]

If the chairman and chief executive are the same person, then the responsibility for checks and balances upon that individual's power will fall largely to the independent non-executive directors. It also makes for a greater need for board committees that can exercise this role of applying an independent-minded review and there is a strong case for a risk committee as well as the three other committees dealt with in the Code. Further, it increases the argument for the non-executive directors to meet together without the presence of chairman or chief executive.

The chairman's role, as discussed previously, is to manage the board but, in doing so, the Code of Corporate Governance refers frequently to specific governance responsibilities of the chairman.

Company secretary

The role of company secretary is no longer a legal requirement for private companies,[2] but many will still have one because of the importance of the role described here. Where it exists, the company secretary is responsible for many of the legal, contractual and administrative duties within the company, including:

- shareholders' register
- register of charges
- register of directors' interests.

The company secretary is the focal point for directors and senior executives to clear their share dealings and sometimes has delegated authority to authorise these.

Although the role is sometimes combined with that of a finance director or of a property director, this is not regarded as 'best practice' except for small companies. This is because the role is important in corporate governance and may incur a conflict of interest if the individual is also a board member.

The company secretary usually prepares the board agenda with the chairman, administers and attends board meetings and prepares minutes. An interest-

[1] Corporate Governance Code. SA.2.1.
[2] Companies Act 2006 S270(1).

ing insight to preparing board minutes was offered by Sir Adrian Cadbury, who observed that '…they ensure that they record the board's decisions, but offer no hostages to fortune should they be called in evidence by any of the regulatory authorities'.[3] This approach has become less common in recent years due to situations in which individual directors, or boards as a whole, want to be able to demonstrate that they have discussed issues, taken an active part in discussions or taken appropriate actions. Board evaluations,[4] for instance, will look at board minutes to assess the contribution of each director; and the FSA, for example, in reviewing directors' 'fit and proper' status will look at their contribution to board meetings through examining the minutes. An important caveat to this approach of producing more informative minutes is for companies with US activities, where fear of US litigation processes may limit the information recorded. Minutes must be kept of all directors' meetings and retained for at least 10 years.[5]

The Corporate Governance Code advises that the appointment and removal of the company secretary should be a matter for the board as a whole.[6] This represents a change whereby this function does not, as is usual for the directors, report to the managing director but is responsible to the board as a whole.

The company secretary is, under the Code, responsible for 'advising the board through the chairman on all governance matters'[7] and is usually the authority on governance and compliance and, even if not legally qualified, will often advise directors on Company Law and Listing requirements. They will communicate to Companies House changes to directors and their details, share capital, company name and registered office and ensure that public documents are available for inspection. They often take responsibility for matters such as property administration and insurance. They will usually administer shareholder communications. They will often work with the chairman and finance director on the company accounts and, for companies that hold one, will administer the AGM.[8]

Corporate governance below board level

The reason for the concentration of work on corporate governance at board level is that the board is both formally responsible for setting policies but is also responsible for ensuring they are followed, which they do through their control of:

[3] Sir Adrian Cadbury (2002) *Corporate Governance and Chairmanship*, Oxford University Press, 129.

[4] Corporate Governance Code. SB6.

[5] Companies Act 2006 S248(2).

[6] Corporate Governance Code SB.5.2.

[7] ibid. SB5.

[8] AGMs are no longer compulsory for private companies unless it is a requirement of their Articles of Association (CA 2006).

- organisation structure
- processes and procedures
- appointments
- communication.

The Code states that 'Corporate governance is therefore about what the board of a company does and how it sets the values of the company, and is to be distinguished from the day to day operational management of the company carried out by full-time executives.'[9] I think this is fundamentally misconceived. It is immaterial if the board has wise and appropriate policies if they are not put into practice by operational management, whether they also sit on the board or not. This is an issue of supervision and control, which is one of the key tasks of the board of any organisation. The sort of problems that arise from a breakdown of control are:

- price fixing
- discrimination in employment and promotion on the basis of race, religion, sex, age, etc.
- bullying
- bribing of local officials
- failure to adhere to health and safety requirements.

There may be others that also run counter to the proclaimed values of the organisation. But all of these failures of governance carry heavy potential costs to businesses. Some of them are public: UK courts can impose fines up to 10% of worldwide turnover for price fixing; discrimination suits tie up management resources in court and can result in substantial fines; bribery is now unlawful even when it takes place abroad. Some of the costs are hidden, but they still damage businesses: bullying and discrimination impair business effectiveness; employees are demoralised and less efficient and good staff leave; individuals agree to report incorrect data or implement policies they know to be wrong. Amongst the hidden costs should also be listed serious reputational damage, which has real-world impact in terms of reduced sales, increased difficulty in recruiting, increased difficulty in forging business partnerships, etc.

It is probably too soon to list causes of the blowout at BP's Deepwater oil platform in 2010 with certainty and accuracy. The leakage of, maybe, 4m barrels of oil was a terrible human, environmental, financial and reputational disaster. However, one of the important elements of corporate governance is 'risk management' and it must be undeniable that BP did not pay sufficient attention to these potential risks. This follows from the sheer scale of the financial cost to BP of this accident at around £20bn, from a blowout at an oil rig being a risk

[9] Corporate Governance Code, Governance and the Code, para 3.

that any rational person would recognise, and finally from published reports that some people knew that some equipment on the rig was not in full working order. Even if responsibility turns out not to lie with BP, a large portion of the costs will lie there and therefore the governance issue of risk management also lies there.

Failure to avoid the occurrence of these unwanted problems is generally down to a failure of management. Directors, once they reach the boards of their companies, are prone to forget that they are still managers and must manage the teams that report to them. As Janice Caplan describes in her book *The Value of Talent*,[10] when they ignore this aspect of their role it often gives rise to a 'disconnect' between the top level of management and those who actually carry out operational roles. This results in a breakdown in information passing up the chain of command, so that the directors do not actually know the detail of what is happening below them; it also results in a breakdown in information and instructions down the chain of command: the operational management can feel unsupported, left to 'swing in the wind'. Thus potentially excellent policies espoused at the top simply stay there and have little effect on what actually happens. The conclusion we must draw from this is that executive directors, just like other managers, must actively manage their team.

There are also positive management actions that can and do create a breakdown in corporate governance.

Discouragement of bad news

In many businesses managers who try to relay bad news are slapped down: this is asking for trouble.

The problems of the Toyota Motor Corporation in 2009 exemplify this problem. The company was forced to recall cars in the USA by the National Highway Traffic Safety Administration, as a result of reports of uncontrollable acceleration. It turned out that dealers and employees had been reporting problems over several years that had been ignored. The company that had been an exemplar for good management and communication and customer centredness proved to have been failing in just these areas of apparent strength.

I came across the problem personally, when I was sitting on a board, and the finance director reported a gross margin that was lower than the chairman wanted to hear. There followed a long, careful and emphatic explanation from the chairman, together with illustrative figures, of why the reported figure could not possibly be correct. He demanded a restatement of the figures, which was done, after the meeting. My only personal defence for not speaking up is that I was new and did not know that the chairman was wrong and the finance director was right, though even at the time it seemed to me that slapping down the finance director did not seem like wise management. About a year later the business failed.

[10] Janice Caplan (2010) *The Value of Talent*, Kogan Page.

If bad news is not acceptable, then it is not given and alternative explanations are found for undeniable facts; and figures are made up.

Unrealistic targets

When the board sets unrealistic targets, then the operational managers have little choice between finding alternative employment and falsifying the figures. They may not do this overtly: they may persuade themselves the figures are correct. The boundary between setting targets that stretches management and encourages them to find new ways of doing things, on the one hand, and being unrealistic, on the other, is a fine one. I have worked in organisations where budgets were rejected and reworked. The process can be successful, but it demands close engagement by the people at the top with their management teams to agree specific actions that will make a difference. In most cases within my experience, this did not happen and the operational management simply made more optimistic assumptions. This is not just a breakdown of management processes: it is poor governance. It means that the systems and procedures by which an organisation is managed do not work.

Excessive rewards

Excessive performance rewards can have the same effect as unrealistic targets. People who stand to make a great deal of money are motivated to find creative ways to attain their targets if reality will not do. The collapse of Barings Bank through the activities of Nick Leeson exemplifies this, even though it was also more complicated. As well as being highly financially motivated to report good figures, Leeson feared the consequences of failure, was not closely supervised on a personal level and was also permitted to manage both the back office and front office of his branch – an obvious breakdown of the checks and balances of good governance.

Resentment of senior management

When poor management creates resentment and sets a bad example, then individuals are far more likely to flout controls, to be cavalier about compliance or to cross the border into falsification. When directors and senior managers are seen to take rewards from their businesses that their staff see as outrageous, then that impacts on loyalty: and loyalty is one of the instruments of good governance. When they are seen to act inappropriately, then they cannot expect that their staff will not follow their example. If this is true of bullying or discriminatory behaviour, then can we expect it not to be true of dishonesty? Examples from the top – for good and bad – cascade down the organisation.

Whistleblowing

Whistleblowing is when someone within an organisation alerts an authority to malpractice. That authority may be within the organisation but outside the usual chain of command; more often it is outside the organisation. The matter complained of is always malpractice because, if it were not, a simple report through the usual chain of command would resolve it.

Why does whistleblowing matter? Because staff within a company may become aware of improprieties at any level of the organisation and, without an effective mechanism in place to act upon such knowledge, this may affect its future success or even survival. Consider, for example, an individual becoming aware of health and safety shortcomings: without corrective action, these might lead to a serious accident, with significant human and financial consequences. Or consider knowledge of fraud or of price-fixing with competitors: such illegal acts can result in heavy fines, civil actions and reputational damage when they eventually come to light.

In an internet age, and one in which tax authorities and regulators take an interest even in anonymous denunciations, it is far better for companies themselves to take control of such matters than to risk losing control.

 In January 2001 Scott Sullivan, chief financial officer of Worldcom, a major US telecommunications business, was under pressure as it became clear that bad debts and falling sales volumes would mean a significant reduction in published earnings. He asked an immediate subordinate to reclassify expenses as capital. Perhaps fearful for his job, that individual agreed and passed the instruction, in turn, to one of his subordinates. All three eventually suffered the repercussions when Worldcom failed.

🗒 *Briefing Lessons*

- **Facing up to a problem immediately, even if the consequences are bad, will usually have a better outcome than covering them over.**
- **Committing a first, minor, impropriety makes the next, bigger one, easier. It also makes it harder to avoid: you must cover up the first one.**

The UK's Public Interest Disclosure Act 1998 (PIDA) provides a framework of legal protection for individuals against victimisation and dismissal if they disclose information that exposes malpractice as well as failure in areas such as health and safety. The legislation followed enquiries into disasters and crimes where employees could have prevented the occurrence had they felt that they would receive support in raising allegations.

The scope of the Act extends to the raising of 'genuine concerns about crime, civil offences (including negligence, breach of contract, breach of administrative law), miscarriage of justice, danger to health and safety or the environment and the cover up of any of these' and extends to all employees in almost all professions; some, such as the army, are excluded. Protection is available through the industrial tribunal system; remedies include unlimited financial compensation and ordering companies to reinstate employees to their role.

It is good practice, and a requirement of the Code,[11] for employers to establish procedures for whistleblowers to air their concerns because otherwise they may feel that public disclosure is their only option, which may then be protected under the Act (s. 43G(3)(f)). Companies should see mechanisms for employees to express concerns outside the normal chain of command as an important element of internal control. Indeed, this approach is illustrated by the ICAEW recommendations[12] that boards should review their whistleblowing arrangements and, in doing so, should ask the following questions:

- Is there evidence that the board regularly considers whistleblowing procedures as part of its review of the system of internal control?
- Are there issues or incidents which have otherwise come to the board's attention which they would have expected to have been raised earlier under the company's whistleblowing procedures?
- Where appropriate, has the internal audit function performed any work that provides additional assurance on the effectiveness of the whistleblowing procedures?
- Are there adequate procedures to track the actions taken in relation to concerns made and to ensure appropriate follow-up action has been taken to investigate and, if necessary, resolve problems indicated by whistleblowing?
- Are there adequate procedures for retaining evidence in relation to each concern?
- Have confidentiality issues been handled effectively?
- Is there evidence of timely and constructive feedback?
- Have any events come to the committee's or the board's attention that might indicate that a staff member has not been fairly treated as a result of their raising concerns?
- Is a review of staff awareness of the procedures needed?

The Code requires audit committees to check on such arrangements and the Smith Report expanded on this issue, saying 'the audit committee should review

[11] Corporate Governance Code SC.3.4.
[12] ICAEW (2004) *Guidance for Audit Committees: whistleblowing arrangements*.

arrangements by which staff of the company may, in confidence, raise concerns about possible improprieties in financial reporting, financial control or any other matters. The audit committee's objective should be to ensure that arrangements are in place for the proportionate and independent investigation of such matters and for appropriate follow up-action, and that any matters relevant to its own responsibilities are brought to its attention.'[13]

The importance of informal channels of communication is illustrated by a famous saying attributed to the British parliamentarian, Edmund Burke:

> All that is necessary for the triumph of evil is that good men do nothing.

But if those who could communicate concerns to the board feel they will be punished as a result, then they may not act or they may see their first option as a denunciation to the authorities. The Nolan Committee enquiring into standards in public life also felt that provision for whistleblowing by employees has benefits to the organisation 'both as an instrument of good governance and a manifestation of a more open culture'.[14] Complaints are not uncommon: in 2008/9 there were 1,761 applications under the PIDA legislation.

Whistleblowing procedures

Companies should make clear to their employees what to do if they come across malpractice in the workplace. This should encourage them to inform someone who has the ability to do something about the problem, but the precise route to follow will depend upon the particular circumstances of different organisations. It will usually be separate from the grievance procedure because the employee may have no personal grievance against the organisation and because of the potentially severe risk to the organisation that these complaints may raise.

> The essence of a whistleblowing system is that staff should be able to bypass the direct management line because that may well be the area about which their concerns arise, and they should be able to go outside the organisation if they feel the overall management is engaged in an improper course.[15]

Guidance on whistleblowing procedures should encompass the following areas:

[13] Robert Smith (2003) *Audit Committees: Combined Code Guidance*, FRC, S5.9

[14] Report of the Committee on Standards in Public Life, quoted in Public Concern at Work (2008) *Whistleblowing Best Practice*.

[15] ibid.

Statement to all employees

This statement should:

- describe the kinds of matter covered by the procedure, ideally giving examples
- state that company policy is that an employee who has reported or is considering reporting an issue of concern under the procedure should never be treated less favourably by any other employee: a breach of this requirement or a malicious complaint constituting a disciplinary offence.

Statement to supervisors and managers

This should outline the requirement to:

- give proper consideration to a complaint under these procedures
- keep a record of complaints
- respond to the complainant with reasons within a specified reasonable period
- report complaints that raise serious matters or require further action to a more senior manager, compliance officer or internal auditor.

Who to contact and how to make a complaint

- The seriousness of the issue will normally influence who is to be contacted with increasing seriousness. The initial contact should be the line manager or their line manager.
- There should be a secondary contact route through designated persons if the complaint concerns the line management or if it is not dealt with properly. These may include:
  - a senior manager
  - a compliance officer
  - internal audit department
  - a designated company director, company secretary, etc.
- There should be an option to raise a complaint in writing and to receive a response in writing to a requested address, together with an undertaking as to how quickly a response will be given.
- The requirement to keep a record of the matter complained about, where and when it occurred and also to whom the complaint was made, how, when and where should be emphasised.

Public Interest Disclosure Act (PIDA) 1998

The guidelines should:

- explain the protection afforded by the PIDA 1998
- emphasise that it covers issues raised in good faith and believed to be true but does not protect anyone who is acting maliciously, making false allegations or who is seeking personal gain
- explain that anonymous complaints may make investigation more difficult but will still be looked at
- offer steps to protect a complainant's identity if required but make clear that a complainant may be requested to act as a witness if disciplinary or other proceedings follow investigation of the issues raised
- make clear that it may be impossible to protect an individual's identity if criminal or other legal charges result.
- In the event that a complainant feels subsequently discriminated against, guidance should provide an internal route to report this.
- Guidance should explain what happens for employees who are the subject of a complaint under the procedure.
- Guidance should list external bodies, to be contacted if response to an internal complaint is unsatisfactory or if an internal complaint would be inappropriate. These may include the company auditor and would include prescribed persons[16] (under the Act) who may receive disclosures without breaching confidentiality. Some companies provide access via a confidential helpline to external advisers such as Public Concern at Work, the whistleblowing charity.

  Despite often showing great courage and determination, whistleblowers are not necessarily popular with their colleagues, particularly where the disclosure threatens people's jobs. HR managers have a duty to support whistleblowers who act in good faith and it is in the long-term interests of the organisation that they should do so.[17]

The practical implementation of these policies is critical and Public Concern at Work has recommended that organisations should ensure that staff are aware of and trust the whistleblowing avenues and should continually review how the procedures work in practice.[18]

[16] See list at http://www.direct.gov.uk/prod_consum_dg/groups/dg_digitalassets/@dg/@en/@employ/documents/digitalasset/dg_177605.pdf.

[17] Chartered Institute of Personnel and Development (CIPD) http://www.cipd.co.uk/subjects/empreltns/whistleblw/whistle.htm.

[18] Public Concern at Work (2008) *Whistleblowing Best Practice*.

Corporate governance: measuring, justifying and promoting

11

Introduction

An old saying in business, which comes in various forms, is often expressed along the lines of 'you can only manage it if you can measure it'. Whilst the universal truth of this can be debated, most people would agree on the importance of trying to measure actions and their results, either directly or indirectly, in order to gauge whether management actions are having an effect. There has therefore been considerable effort made to assess and measure corporate governance with a view to justifying doing it and also to support the promotion of good governance practice to stakeholders.

How to measure corporate governance

There is no generally agreed method for measuring corporate governance and attempts to create one can be very subjective. Nonetheless, the Association of British Insurers set up a database of quoted companies in 1993 that has collected data on compliance with the Combined Code and with what it views as best practice, as set out in ABI Guidelines. Around 40 indicators are measured. Breaches of these best practice indicators are scored by red top indicating serious concern, amber less so and blue the lowest level. Results and a detailed report are available through its Institutional Voting Information System.[1]

There are two problems with a methodology of this sort.

- **Tick-box approach** – The system gives the same weight to what might be viewed as important or unimportant indicators although, by publishing raw data, the IVIS system allows the user to apply their own value judgements and to draw their own conclusions.

- **Missing ingredients** – Information that is used for measurements could be wrong as a result of failure by employees to report properly. Whilst there is apparently no way of protecting measurement systems from such inaccuracy, I would argue that good governance in the first place makes such failures more difficult to perpetrate subsequently. This means that other indicators of the quality of governance may suggest the overall level of risk.

The failure of Enron was the largest corporate bankruptcy in US history up to that time and one of the most prominent cases of corporate malpractice for many years. The board was unaware that Kopper, one of the company's employees, was its partner in a company called Chewco that was set up as an off-balance sheet financing vehicle.

---

[1] www.ivis.co.uk.

The minutes and the interviews we conducted do not reveal any disclosure to the Executive Committee of Kopper's role, and they do not indicate that the Executive Committee (or Lay) was asked for or made the finding necessary under Enron's Code of Conduct to permit Kopper to have a financial interest in Chewco. Both Fastow and Kopper participated in the telephonic meeting. Each had an obligation to bring Kopper's role to the committee's attention.[2]

So systems were in place but were abused? They were, but the failure to volunteer information would have been much more difficult if good corporate governance procedures had been followed elsewhere:

- *The CEO and chairman were the same person, as is fairly common in US companies.*
- *The board had countenanced a different instance of employee participation in a special-purpose entity which gave rise to a conflict of interest. If that had been refused, it would have set a clear boundary of acceptability which might have influenced disclosure by employees and auditors.*
- *The board was aware of the use of off-balance sheet financing even if unaware of the nature of the risks involved.[3]*
- *Employee remuneration was highly sensitive to the company share price, and the element of remuneration that was not fixed was not linked to long-term performance.*

 Briefing Lessons

- **The first departure from good governance may lead to others.**
- **Once you countenance an instance of unethical behaviour you lower the bar for other instances.**

Systems of measurement examine published information and have no way of measuring corporate culture or how well the board actually functions; it could outwardly comply with best practice yet be inwardly dysfunctional. A US Senate investigation into the Enron affair heard that:

---

[2] Report by the Special Investigative Committee of the Board of Directors of Enron Corp, 1 Feb 2002, http://news.findlaw.com/hdocs/docs/enron/sicreport/index.html.

[3] Robert Rosen (2003) 'Risk management and corporate covernance: the case of Enron', *Connecticut Law Review*, **35**(1157) 1170, http://papers.ssrn.com/sol3/papers.cfm?abstract_id=468168.

...the directors argued that management misled and concealed facts about the company's activities from them, the board in fact had substantial amounts of information about the high risk accounting and structured finance vehicles used by Enron. And instead of responding with probing questions to what corporate governance and accounting experts...characterized as obvious red flags, the board simply and unreasonably (in light of the warning signs) relied on management. Indeed the board and its committees met only five times annually and spent under an hour examining even the most complicated transactions. [4]

Whilst UK codes require publication of the number of board and committee meetings held annually, they cannot specify that directors ask pertinent questions. The corporate governance codes of conduct in the UK employ a 'comply or explain' system that requires companies to report on why they have not followed a particular recommendation. This opens the way for directors themselves or for outside observers to follow the example of the ABI and to see where a company does not follow best practice and to judge whether this seems reasonable in the circumstances. The answer is unlikely to be a score but may be a judgement that, on balance, a particular company does or does not enjoy good governance.

How to justify addressing corporate governance – the business case

There are two stages to making a business case for good corporate governance. The first is to list some of the consequences of poor governance and the second is to look at how those may affect the organisation.

Consequences of poor governance

The more important adverse consequences of poor corporate governance are:

- Weak board effectiveness:
  - errors in direction
  - failure of control
- Fraud, conflicts of interest
- Influence within the organisation of receiving a poor example:
  - poor morale
  - copying of behaviour seen in others – fraud, theft, conflicts of interest, bullying, misinformation

---

[4] Report of the Staff to the Senate Committee on Governmental Affairs, October 2002, http://hsgac.senate.gov/100702watchdogsreport.pdf.

- Failure to observe organisational policy, leading to:
  - unlawful behaviour
  - inappropriate behaviour
  - unauthorised actions
- Failure of accurate and timely transmission of information:
  - within the organisation
  - to external stakeholders.

These consequences then lead to three broad business justifications for good corporate governance. The first is the public case, or externalities.

Externalities

An important argument for improving corporate governance is that, as a society, we have no choice. Economists refer to effects that are outside the particular economic system being studied as 'externalities'. There are significant effects of corporate scandals and failures that are external to the companies concerned and impose costs on the entire community. This has been illustrated by Bruno Cova, former chief counsel for the administrator of Parmalat.[5] In a presentation in 2005 he

> ..underscored how the effects of financial fraud can extend far beyond the direct losses suffered by a company, its shareholders, employees and suppliers. Frauds of this nature erode corporate trust and destabilize global financial markets. A domino effect occurs as investments decrease, market liquidity is squeezed, and increased bankruptcies push the cost of borrowing higher for companies not directly related to the frauds. The cost of doing business increases as new regulation aimed at stopping further frauds takes effect. The way of doing business changes, for the worse.

> Not only do the financial and corporate sectors suffer as a result of large-scale financial fraud. People lose their jobs, pension funds suffer, social costs spiral, and the resulting public outrage can lead to political unrest.[6]

Such frauds, if they are detected, may have simply deferred business failures that would have occurred anyway, meaning that the costs to society have not been increased. Moreover, if they are not detected, that can only be because the business problems were short-term and there is no economic loss to society.

[5] Parmalat is an Italian food conglomerate that grew dramatically through acquisitions in the 1990s only to collapse in 2003 when a £4bn accounting fraud was revealed.

[6] International Chamber of Commerce Commercial Crime Services, 2005. http://www. icc-ccs.org/index.php?option=com_content&view=article&id=100:parmalat-scandal-examined-at-ccs-lecture-series&catid=60:news&Itemid=51.

However, if public and business confidence is eroded, then that has a real and permanent impact on the economy and on people's lives. This means that governments have a significant interest in improving corporate governance and will do so by regulation and enforcement if it cannot be achieved through voluntary codes of conduct.

The problem is also increasingly significant because of the growing scale of business enterprises around the world and their inter-connectedness. Once, a failure like Lehman Brothers in 2006 would have been a serious local issue but, with both subsidiaries and thousands of counterparties to transactions spread around the world, it has had a serious global effect on banking and business confidence. Some scholars have claimed to have detected a real slowdown in business as a result of Enron.

The threat is that, if organisations do not do corporate governance voluntarily, then governments and regulators will do it to them. Most business organisations feel that tight government regulation clamps down on (the good sort) of ingenuity and flexibility in business, increases costs through the need for compliance mechanisms and does not even work very effectively. As an example, it is argued that tight US regulation that followed the Enron and Worldcom failures has created a huge mass of rules that companies devote a great deal of ingenuity to subverting. Whilst the externalities largely arise from scandals at big public companies, the regulation would be likely to apply broadly and far down the size scale.

Punishments

The second business justification is fear of punishment for failure. Companies suffer severe penalties for poor governance that leads to the punishments of:

- fines
- forced business change
- civil court action
- reputational damage
- business failure.

Serious fines may be imposed by courts for governance failures that lead to price-fixing, monopolist behaviour, bribery, breaches of health and safety legislation, etc. In some instances of monopolist behaviour, businesses may be forced to dispose of parts of their businesses. Civil action from authorities, businesses or individuals alleging wrongful behaviour can also comprise an expensive punishment. Damage to the reputation of a business may result from publicity relating to any of the three possible sources of punishment listed above but, of course, it may also result from behaviour that was perfectly lawful but unpopular. If such behaviour was contrary to company policy but occurred anyway then that is a governance issue. Such damage may often have a financial cost as well, if some customers turn away and sales are lost. Where, for example, some shareholders are seen to gain what is perceived as an advantage over other shareholders or over other stakeholders, then there may be a future cost as suppliers refuse to supply, financiers or advisers refuse to act. The final and also the ultimate punishment comes from the markets that businesses trade in. As an example, governance issues frequently arise from a dominant director pushing through a policy or an acquisition without proper challenge or questioning from other directors and in extreme, but often very public, cases this may result in substantial losses or even bankruptcy.

Efficiency and effectiveness

Can it be shown that good governance improves organisational efficiency and effectiveness? I think it does but it is hard to prove. As outlined under Does good governance work? in Chapter 3, the statistical evidence from markets is weak, but this may be partly because it is hard to know exactly what to measure. It may be hard to know which elements of good governance matter most, which not at all, and how the presence of one element may compensate for the absence of another or whether having two particular elements together creates a larger effect than adding the effect of each on its own.

How to talk about corporate governance

The key audiences to speak to about corporate governance are:

- fellow directors or senior executives
- employees
- shareholders
- other stakeholders.

I have discussed throughout this book why good corporate governance matters; but I have also stressed that it is achieved not just through systems and procedures but also through behaviours. It is therefore essential that governance is discussed and genuinely supported at a senior level and that this is not just lip-service. There must be a business vision at board level that includes values that are lived, not just suffered, an ethical approach and a commitment to best practice.

In making good governance work, there is no magic bullet. It demands three elements:

- commitment at the top
- each executive level acting as role model for their direct reports
- company values and vision must continually be communicated.

There must be commitment to ensure little lapses are not tolerated because those escalate into big lapses. Acting as a role model means no shared jokes about 'silly rules', accompanied by connivance at rule breaking. And company values on a range of matters, such as ethics, health and safety, control systems, etc., must be spoken about and clearly communicated throughout the organisation. The language must be everyday speech and specific, not vague generalities that people laugh at and ignore or that can be interpreted in diverse ways. Reasons for procedures must be given and explained.

The UK Corporate Governance Code requires companies to report on their corporate governance in a number of ways, which should cover:

- a statement of how the board operates, including a high-level statement of which types of decisions are to be taken by the board and which are delegated to management
- the names of the non-executive directors whom the board determines to be independent, with reasons where necessary
- a statement of how performance evaluation of the board, its committees and its directors has been conducted
- terms of reference of board committees.

Whilst some of this must be communicated through the Directors Report, some can be done through a company website. Oddly, the FSA, as listing authority for the London Stock Exchange (LSE), imposes no requirements for a company website whilst AIM,[7] run by the LSE itself, requires companies to make key company information available on a website,[8] which must be best practice for any company. A website must also, surely, be a key element of communication with stakeholders, providing a cheap and easy way to meet regulatory obligations, to promote a brand image and communicate equally with customers, suppliers, employees (and potential employees), shareholders and the wider community.

The full AIM rule can be found on the LSE website.[9] This is a communication opportunity, and a guidance note is provided by the QCA[10] and also by the Investor Relations Society.[11] Best practice extracted from these suggests companies should provide:

- description of the business and its main operations
- names, brief biographies and description of responsibilities of directors

[7] Alternative Investment Market, the junior market run by The London Stock Exchange.

[8] AIM Rule 26. AIM requires posting of the most recent admission document, but this risks interpretation by the US authorities as soliciting investment.

[9] http://www.londonstockexchange.com.

[10] QCA (2007) *AIM Website Guide – Rule 26*.

[11] http://www.ir-soc.org.uk.

- Articles of Association
- at least the most recent annual report and subsequent interim reports
- any company announcements
- recent shareholder circulars.

Usefully, the QCA guide emphasises the need to make websites accessible to people suffering from disabilities and recommends further guidance from organisations such as the 'Web Access Initiative'[12] and RNIB.[13]

Best practice suggests that all governance issues should be accessible through one website page so that even if detail is located in different places it can be reached through hyperlinks.

[12] http://www.w3.org/WAI/resources.
[13] http://www.rnib.org.uk.

[PART THREE]

Intervention

Executive intervention

12

Introduction

I am going beyond executive intervention here to consider a wider range of stakeholders who may intervene to influence corporate governance because non-directors and more junior staff can definitely have an interventionary role as part of the enterprise, as do investors.

What are the make-or-break decisions?

Boards constantly make critical decisions relating to their two key functional areas of:

- strategy and direction
- supervision and control.

Matters of strategy and direction are clearly critical to businesses but they do not normally give rise to governance issues except in relation to the process by which those decisions are taken. So ensuring that these are supported by adequate information reaching the board and that appropriate authority is delegated and appropriate conditions attached are all crucial. The sort of specific decisions covered will include:

- acquisitions and disposals
- capital investment
- major human resource questions.

Decisions that relate to supervision and control often involve issues of corporate governance. There are too many detailed decisions to list, but the three most important categories that these critical decisions fall into are:

- internal communication
- delegated authority
- risk management.

However, it is also important to refer to a class of make-or-break decisions that may be made by individuals at any level within a company:

- whistleblowing.

Internal communication

Time and again, the successes and failures of supervision in organisations come down to flows of information up and down the hierarchy. Proper control of such flows includes establishing a culture where problems and bad news are communicated effectively up the chain of command; it also includes having internal mechanisms to bypass that chain of command in the event that there is a blockage that stops the flow.

 GlaxoSmithKline is one of the biggest drug companies in the world. In 2002, it sent Cheryl Eckard, a global quality assurance manager, to their Puerto Rican plant to fix manufacturing violations that had been cited by the US Federal Drug Administration. She found problems that went far beyond these violations and tried to raise her concerns with superiors, including making a full report to GSK's Compliance Department. Instead of escalating the internal investigation, GSK fired Eckard in May 2003. Even subsequent to this, Eckard tried to call the then chief executive, who would not take her call. As a result of her failure to get her reports investigated properly, she reported the matter to the Federal Drug Administration (FDA) and subsequently filed suit against GSK on behalf of the US government under the US False Claims Act, which allows individuals to sue suppliers to the US government on its behalf and to receive a share of any recovery. In 2009, the plant was closed and in 2010, after nearly seven years, GSK settled this claim for $750m. The company 'declined to say whether further lawsuits from patients may be expected'.[1]

It is interesting to note that GSK's report on its corporate governance in its annual report and accounts is a model of compliance; and yet what is described above is a gross failure of governance, of which there is no mention.

 Briefing Lessons

- **Having procedures that ensure employee concerns are properly investigated and passed up the organisation is a first step.**
- **Having a culture that will not cover up problems is a necessary second step.**
- **On top of those necessary steps the board has a duty of supervision, to ensure these processes actually work.**

---

[1] Simon Goodley (2010), 'GlaxoSmithKline whistleblower wins record £61m payout', *The Guardian*, 27 October.

Delegated authority

This idea of delegation covers three related make-or-break decisions, including:

- appointing individuals to key executive roles
- choosing how to delegate authority
- supervising how authority is used.

The example of GEC, discussed below, illustrates how disastrous it can be to choose the wrong people. Yet the selection process is a difficult one, seeking to assess competence and integrity in a situation that is probably new to that individual. You may be extrapolating from known performance in a previous role to unknown performance in a completely new role as well, which is even harder. The alternative of using people who have done the same job before may be unavailable and may be undesirable because it limits innovation, without which organisations cannot grow and adapt.

The amount of authority delegated and ensuring it is shared with others can impose a constraint that limits risk to the organisation. Examples of this may include delegating authority to a committee or requiring two signatories on a cheque. In some instances, delegation may be partial, so a chief executive may be authorised to negotiate an acquisition or a major contract but be required to make any agreement subject to board approval.

Shared authority and partial delegation are not always possible and, in the end, it is always up to the board to supervise how authority is used, once granted. This means that the executive must report back to the board at appropriate intervals on progress, details and results.

Risk management

The board is responsible for determining the nature and extent of the significant risks it is willing to take in achieving its strategic objectives.[2]

Arnold Weinstock was a smart accountant who married the boss's daughter and advanced to running the business. He engineered a reverse takeover of GEC, one of the UK's great electrical and engineering companies that dated back to the 1880s. The business had faltered, but Weinstock cut back and rationalised, returning it to profit and then followed this with a series of astute takeovers that rapidly turned GEC into an industrial giant. His penchant for cost and financial control was legendary, personally reviewing detailed figures for his businesses and interrogating his managers on the details, line by line. However, over time, he became increasingly cautious and risk averse, amassing a much criticised £3bn cash mountain rather than either investing in new projects or returning the money to shareholders.

[2] The Corporate Governance Code, Main Principle C2.

Weinstock retired in 1996 and installed George Simpson as his successor. An industrialist with a background at the top of Rover Group and British Aerospace, he was expected to revive GEC from its last years of caution and torpor. However, he did this rather more energetically than might have been imagined, deciding to refocus the company totally as a telecommunications and electronics company serving the burgeoning internet markets. Over just three years he sold off old engineering businesses and invested heavily in buying internet businesses. Investors liked the new strategy and, under his command, the share price rocketed from £3 to £12 but there were nagging critics of the strategy. US-based analysts, in particular, wondered whether GEC (renamed Marconi) was late in the game and too small to compete with the US giants. Some £4.5bn was spent in a series of acquisitions at the top of the market. When the market faltered in 2000 GEC imploded. By mid-2001 the share price had fallen to £1 and the cash mountain had been replaced with debt approaching the same size. Simpson left shortly after. By 2005 the last bits of this great business had been sold off.

It is hard to imagine that the board thought clearly about the level of risk it wanted to take because, all at the same time, it accepted risks relating to:

- *new strategy*
- *new markets*
- *concentration*
- *acquisition*
- *financial structure.*

Business involves risk, but adopting a new strategy of single-minded focus on a completely new market (new to it but also not having existed for long) through acquisition whilst abandoning old businesses and racking up huge debts must be an all-time risk record.

 Briefing Lesson

- **It is important to bear in mind that taking risks that do not pay off can have disastrous consequences.**

The Code states that 'the board should, at least annually, conduct a review of the effectiveness of the company's risk management and internal control systems',[3] whilst the Companies Act requires, except for companies subject to the small companies' regime, publication of a directors report that includes a review containing 'a description of the principal risks and uncertainties facing the company.'[4]

[3] Corporate Governance Code SC.2.1.
[4] Companies Act 2006 S417(3b).

Referring back to the example of GSK, discussed in the previous section, the company's risk management system is discussed at length in their annual report, including diagrams of committee reporting and, as regards the Code, it ticks all the boxes. Indeed, the list of principal risks conveys a strong understanding of the business environment, except that there is no reference to employees covering up bad news or failing to pass on information or of provision for internal whistle-blowing. And this, despite the company being involved in a $750m court case.

 Briefing Lesson

- **The make-or-break decisions include taking risk management seriously and doing more than just ticking boxes.**

The King Report[5] argues that where a company has an internal audit department, its report to the board on the effectiveness of internal controls should not just measure compliance with procedures but also consider how effectively those controls manage business risks.

A risk management process employed by Inchcape plc involved getting the boards of operating subsidiaries to identify their principal areas of risk and to submit a return to the group head office detailing:

- the main risks
- their likely consequences
- their probability of occurrence
- outline of proposed mitigating actions – to cover reducing the incidence as well as the consequences and 'after the fact' actions.

Thus the process was about disaster management as well as merely information gathering.

One wise additional point made in the Turnbull Guidance on Internal Control is also to consider the 'costs of…controls…relative to the benefit'.[6]

The most difficult part of the process is identifying the biggest risks. There are easy ones, such as fire, flood, loss of computer systems and strikes, but the harder part is getting people to think more widely to less likely problems that might nonetheless have very large consequences. In the case of Inchcape, there was a feedback from head office to complete the process.

Most companies will need to include health and safety amongst the risks considered at board level, both because of the potential consequences of a serious

[5] The Institute of Directors in South Africa (2009) *King Code of Governance Principles*.
[6] FRC (2005) *Internal Control: Revised Guidance for Directors on the Combined Code*, S16.

mishap and because being able to produce evidence of having taken the company's responsibilities seriously at the highest level may form part of a legal defence.

Board consideration of procedures and internal communication to minimise the risk of employees or agents engaging in bribery should also be part of its risk assessment process.

Whistleblowing

The importance to a company of whistleblowing, both as an opportunity and threat, has been discussed elsewhere and the critical decisions relating to it are:

- To authorise procedures:
  - for employees to notify their concerns
  - for investigating those concerns
- To ensure that these systems:
  - are properly communicated
  - work in practice.

When is my intervention needed?

Good corporate governance does not just rely upon adhering to rules or even to principles and guidance set out in various codes. It also relies upon the behaviour of individuals who sit on boards and relies upon them:

- devoting sufficient time
- asking pertinent questions
- being aware of their responsibilities and being courageous.

Intervention is needed when the governance process itself is flawed, such as when directors are given inadequate induction or insufficient information, access to senior management, or support; or when the board does not discuss important issues, does not give them sufficient time or if discussion and decisions are not properly minuted.

Intervention is also required when specific issues arise where one or more directors feel there is a significant governance issue. It is impossible to list every possible material issue but, for example, it may be:

- of an operational nature, where there is inadequate risk assessment of an investment
- relating to shareholder rights where a class of shareholder is to be diluted through disapplication of pre-emption rights
- involving shareholder relations where a director becomes aware of investor concerns.

When thinking about intervention, all directors need to consider the consequences of negligence in the performance of their duties. For example, in relation to the annual report, **each director** must have 'taken all the steps he ought to have taken as a director in order to make himself aware of any relevant audit information and to establish that the company's auditor is aware of that information'.[7] These steps would include making 'such enquiries of his fellow directors and…auditors as are required by his duty…to exercise reasonable skill, care and diligence'. If they were 'reckless as to whether [a statement in the report] was false and failed to take reasonable steps to prevent the report from being approved', then they commit an offence that could incur a fine or imprisonment. So sitting on a board and failing to ask pertinent questions can have consequences beyond damage to an individual's reputation. These issues apply just as much to small private companies as to large public ones.

Beyond the board, good governance also needs people to speak up, going through their chain of command when possible or, when it is not, using alternative procedures such as an internal audit department or compliance department or alerting an independent director. Any step outside procedures prescribed by organisational policies is termed whistleblowing. It does carry the danger of disciplinary action, although they may be protected by PIDA legislation (1998) (see Whistleblowing in Chapter 10).

Revealing and protesting against improper behaviour may range from concerns about health and safety to unlawful or unethical trading practices. Whether the concerned party is a board director or a junior employee, speaking out may have adverse employment consequences and must be done with great care. In particular, the law only protects disclosures made:

- in good faith
- in the *reasonable* belief that the allegation is true [my emphasis]
- not for personal gain

and subject to the proviso that in all the circumstances of the case the disclosure is reasonable.[8]

The Audit Committee must intervene if there are signs that something might be seriously amiss[9] with the accounts or with the control process.

What questions should I ask, and who should I ask?

The key figures in implementing good corporate governance, and who will answer the key questions:

[7] Companies Act 2006 S418.

[8] Public Interest Disclosure Act 1998 S43G.

[9] Robert Smith (2003), *Audit Committees: Combined Code Guidance*, FRC, S1.11.

- The chairman, whose role is to lead and manage the board, set its agenda and ensure its effectiveness.
- The senior independent director, if there is one, who has an important role if the chairman is not independent, perhaps through having been CEO or having had significant previous involvement with the company. The SID acts as a liaison with major shareholders and should be available to receive concerns regarding corporate governance from employees.
- The company secretary, who should become expert on legal requirements for the company and directors and the various codes and guidances. Together with the chairman, the company secretary is responsible for the timely flow of information to the board.

However, although much of the governance process is to challenge the executive team, the chief executive is also an important part of the process.

- The chief executive has a critical role in corporate governance, heading the team that provides information; and because governance starts at board level but cascades down through the organisation.

As well as posing questions at board meetings, much of the detailed work of the board and the key questions are dealt with through the three critical sub-committees: nomination, remuneration, and audit and risk. The important questions may be asked here and directed to outside advisers as much as to the executive. The auditors (and internal auditors for companies that have them) will answer questions posed by the audit committee, which will also discuss issues with the finance director. The remuneration committee will have access to reward consultants and the nominations committee will have access to executive search firms.

Sometimes it is people below board level who control the flow of information to the board, whose members need to ask pertinent questions directly of them to satisfy themselves that they are getting complete and accurate information.

There is an infinity of possible questions a board member may need to ask, but they may be divided into the four roles the board performs and examples include:

- **Direction**
    - Does the company have clear values, vision and objectives and are its strategies likely to fulfil them?
    - Are significant operational, financial and compliance risks assessed?
    - Is there a clear understanding of what level of risks are acceptable?
    - Does the company, and individuals within it, possess the capabilities to achieve the company's objectives and, if not, what plans are in place to address the deficit?
    - Is there an appropriate succession planning process?
    - Do the company's culture and HR policies support business objectives?

- **Supervision**
  - – Are there clear strategies and policies for addressing risks?
  - – Are authority, responsibility and accountability clearly defined?
  - – Are there detailed compliance procedures in place in relation to governance, health and safety, bribery, money laundering, etc.?
  - – When weaknesses and failures are identified, are they and their causes investigated and remedial actions taken?
  - – Do management and the board receive timely, relevant and reliable reports?
  - – Are periodic reports effective in communicating a balanced and comprehensible account of the company's position and prospects?
  - – Are appropriate key performance indicators defined and how is the business performing against them?
  - – Are there established and effective channels of communication for individuals to communicate governance concerns?
  - – Are there processes embedded within the operations, which monitor the application of policies and processes related to internal control and risk management?
  - – Is there effective follow-up to address changed risk assessments?
  - – Is there appropriate communication to the board about the effectiveness of monitoring and procedures and to notify it of specific problems?

- **Decide its members and order its proceedings**
  - – Does the board operate effectively?
  - – Is there an appropriate succession planning process?
  - – Does the board receive appropriate training and development?
  - – Is the remuneration policy and its structure appropriate?

- **Communication**
  - – Does the company effectively communicate its vision, values and shared understanding to its employees?
  - – Is there a regular programme of communication with major shareholders?

Individually, and as a board, directors should have access to independent legal advice. The questions posed to lawyers may cover the range of issues outlined above as well as:

- Are the company's actions lawful?

- What further compliance measures should be taken?

- What are the directors' potential liabilities in following a particular course of action?

- As a director, what are my rights and duties?

What are the decisions I need to make?

Decisions arising from the role as a board member can be separated from those of an executive, even if the same person performs both roles. The board role is seldom to originate a proposal but to decide upon proposals put forward by the executive. This may change in a crisis, such as financial difficulties or a bid approach, when the board takes on a quasi-operational role. For example, financial reporting standards 'require directors to satisfy themselves that it is reasonable for them to conclude whether it is appropriate to prepare financial statements on a going concern basis'.[10] This leads to three possible conclusions:

- There are no material uncertainties that may affect a judgement that the company is a going concern.
- There are material uncertainties, but the going concern basis remains appropriate.
- The use of going concern is not appropriate.

In an extreme situation it will be up to the board to decide upon whether the company can continue to trade. During a bid, documents will need to be approved and decisions on approach and wording taken that do not come up from the executive level: these will need to be approved by each board member.

It is too complex to list every possible governance-oriented decision the board must take in the normal course of business. As a board member, however, there are three main categories of decision to take:

- support an executive proposal
- oppose an executive proposal
- seek further information.

Challenging consensual thinking can be difficult and can strain relationships when a board needs to operate on mutual respect and trust. However, being a board member demands courage as a main attribute – alongside competence.

However, there is another critical class of decision posed to board members:

- remove a board member.

A proposal to remove a chief executive, chairman or finance director will arise at the board level itself and signifies a change in strategic direction or, more rarely, an extreme response to a supervision issue such as poor performance or misconduct.

As a senior executive or, indeed, at any level below board level the critical decisions to take with regard to a governance issue are threefold: whether to obey an instruction, whether to object and whether to convey information about a matter of concern to someone who can take a decision.

[10] FRC (2010) *Going Concern and Liquidity Risk: guidance for directors of UK companies*.

What levers should I pull?

The levers of action that are available depend, of course, on who you are. Someone who feels that 'something needs to be done' can range from a director to a senior executive to a more junior member of staff. It may extend from an investor to an external stakeholder such as a member of the public.

Within the boardroom

Disputes may become personal; they may extend to lobbying outside board meetings and the emergence of factions or to pressure on one or more dissident members. The responsibility for managing such situations lies firmly with the chairman: that is a key aspect of the role. However, if that does not happen satisfactorily, the individual director has a series of options:

- Resolve by group discussion within the meeting.
- Insist upon a specific issue being tabled as an agenda item.
- One-to-one discussion with the disputant outside the meeting.
- Speak to chairman to discuss concerns.
  It is the chairman's job to manage the board. Any director can ask for a matter of dispute to be put to a vote.
- Ensure that concerns are minuted.
  It would be extraordinary if such a request were denied. If it were, then a letter to the chairman, requesting that concerns were minuted, would put the matter on record. This may be a difficult step and is only one step from resignation.
- Speak to the senior independent non-executive director, if there is one, if concerns are not being adequately considered.
- Resign. Listed companies have to announce board resignations through an approved Regulatory Information Service and, in some circumstances, feel bound to give reasons for the resignation. This step should be sufficient to avoid the possible consequences of an improper act by the board.
- Resignation letter. The Code requires that, 'on resignation a non-executive director should provide a written statement for the chairman for circulation to the board, if they have any…concerns'.[11] Whilst only mandatory for listed companies, a private company director can still write to the chairman and request that their letter be circulated.

The Code recommends that directors (it says, 'especially an independent director'[12] but I do not know why there should be a distinction) should have access to external legal advice paid for by the company, where they judge it necessary to discharge their duties as directors.

[11] Corporate Governance Code SA.4.3.
[12] ibid. SB.5.1.

Outside the boardroom

An individual who is not a board member may come across a matter of concern that is related to corporate governance. Examples may range from accounting fraud (which can either involve incorrect reporting or actual theft) to bullying, discrimination, bribery or significant breaches of good health and safety practices. Only the individual can judge whether the issue is serious enough to be pursued beyond an immediate line manager and, if so, how far to escalate it. Options include:

- request written instructions for an action
- refuse to follow an instruction that involves improper behaviour
- register a protest in writing about a matter of concern
- register concerns with someone higher up the chain of command
- register concerns with someone outside the chain of command such as a compliance officer
- convey information to the board
- make a report outside the organisation.

A protest by email leaves an electronic trail and is an extremely effective means of making a protest against any sort of wrongful behaviour. Such complaints by a junior employee at Enron later made it very difficult for senior management to deny that they knew what was going on. A concerned individual should always keep a detailed written record of the steps they take, including where and when a discussion took place, what was said, who was involved and who may have witnessed it.

As an investor

Investors also have an important role in governance. The Stewardship Code[13] refers to seven possible escalations after an initial, and unsatisfied, discussion with the company through its chairman or senior independent director:

- 'holding additional meetings with management specifically to discuss concerns;
- expressing concerns through the company's advisers;
- meeting with the chairman, senior independent director or with all the independent directors;
- intervening jointly with other institutions on particular issues;
- making a public statement in advance of the AGM or an EGM;
- submitting resolutions at shareholders' meetings; and
- requisitioning an EGM, in some cases proposing to change board membership'.

[13] FRC (2010) *UK Stewardship Code*, Principle 4.

In practice, some investors have made their concerns known through the press but, although this is embarrassing, it is unclear whether it is effective in changing behaviours. It is more likely to do so in instances where the company's brand image is important to it.

How do we know when we've succeeded or failed?

There are qualitative and quantitative indications that demonstrate success and failure in corporate governance. The obvious badge of failure occurs when there is a significant problem such as:

- arraignment for legal or regulatory transgression
- dispute with shareholders
- damage to reputation arising from ethical or social responsibility issues
- business problems indicating poor risk management
- employees' actions or behaviours that are contrary to company policy.

However, before such serious events occur, there should be ways to discover whether there are problems that could lead to them and which need to be addressed.

Employee surveys

Good human resource management practice, which has clear business benefits, makes use of employee engagement surveys in order to test morale and highlight problem areas in management that you can do something about, as well as strengths to be reinforced. A properly designed questionnaire, and one that offers confidentiality, will invariably provide an indication of governance issues below board level and, if there are problems here, it implies there may be problems at board level too. For example, a survey of this type might indicate a lack of respect for, trust in or confidence in senior management. There is strong evidence to show that high levels of employee engagement are correlated with improved business performance, so such surveys have a strong business purpose.[14] These are not just management issues, however: they are about governance too. Staff who have low morale are not just under-performing: they are likely to have less loyalty to the organisation and may be more likely to act in ways contrary to company policy or be affected by those above them doing so. Issues that may emerge, for example in relation to communication from and to the board, are directly relevant because board effectiveness is an important objective of corporate governance. Used together with other HR tools, employee engagement

[14] David Macleod and Nita Clarke (2009) *Engaging for Success: enhancing performance through employee engagement*, Department for Business Innovation and Skills.

surveys can provide powerful tools to enhance board and senior management effectiveness.[15]

Whistleblowing procedures

As discussed (see Whistleblowing in Chapter 10), it is in the interests of organisations to have procedures for people who have concerns to be able to raise them. In small organisations that are owner-managed, staff will have immediate access to senior management but, once the organisation grows to a higher level of complexity, there must be a procedure for bypassing the normal reporting to an immediate line manager, if this is not getting anywhere or if the problem is that the manager is behaving inappropriately. Such procedures provide an opportunity for news of problems to reach senior management before they become serious.

Review best practice

The various codes referred to in this book establish a benchmark of best practice. Companies can review whether they are complying with the recommendations. Non-compliance should then raise the question of whether it is appropriate to change practices to comply or whether the organisation's current policies suit its needs and those of stakeholders better. Instances where non-compliance may be appropriate could include combination of the CEO and chairman's role in an owner-managed start-up or early-stage business and also having few or no non-executive directors in such companies.

Evaluation of board and director effectiveness

A regular evaluation process (see Board evaluation in Chapter 6) is one source of evidence for the effectiveness of corporate governance. Ensuring that questions are searching may require some outside facilitation to obtain an independent view and expert knowledge of governance issues and best practice.

Comparison with peers and role models

This too is likely to need some external input, although for the larger companies much can be learnt from reading their published annual report to see what they are doing and how far they are complying with codes and with best practice.

Use of consultancies

Companies often seek outside advice on governance best practice, perhaps also taken with advice on creating a more effective board. There are many independent consultancies as well as those tied to audit practices.

[15] Janice Caplan (2010) *The Value of Talent*, Kogan Page.

Membership of groups and associations

There are a number of organisations, covering businesses, not-for-profit organisations and the public sector, that exist to discuss and promote aspects of corporate governance such as corporate social responsibility or business ethics. Meetings and discussions may also be organised within trade and professional bodies that organisations and executives may belong to. Such forums allow organisations to gauge whether their systems and procedures conform to best practice.

[PART FOUR]

In depth

Additional resources

13

- Online sources
- Courses
- Books

Online sources

The following organisation and website information was accurate at the date of publication. The list is not exhaustive but indicates at least some of the useful resources available on a range of corporate governance issues.

Information of governance

There are many organisations and associations that provide information on governance to the public and not just to their members and subscribers

The Quoted Companies Alliance (QCA)

Represents small and mid-cap quoted companies outside the FTSE 350, including those on AIM and PLUS Markets. There are nearly 2,000 such companies – 85% of all UK quoted companies – employing around 1 million people, generating £3.5 billion of taxes from companies and £5 billion of taxes from employees.
http://www.theqca.com/

EuropeanIssuers

Association whose members are European associations of quoted companies as well as individual companies.
http://www.europeanissuers.eu/en/

The Institute of Directors

Provides a range of information but has, in particular, published a governance code of practice specifically for unlisted companies in November 2010.
http://www.iod.com

The Association of British Insurers

Represents the insurance industry, whose members are believed to account for around 20% of investment in the UK stockmarket by value. They provide best practice guidance through their IVIS website (see below).
http://www.abi.org.uk/

Institutional Voting Information Service

Part of the ABI, provides research and helps members exercise their proxy voting rights. It also hosts the ABI's best practice guidance on governance for investors and companies.
http://www.ivis.co.uk/Guidelines.aspx

Institutional Shareholders Committee

A forum for UK institutional shareholders, also publishes guidance notes.
http://www.institutionalshareholderscommittee.org.uk/index.html

The Pre-Emption Group

Represents listed companies, investors and intermediaries and provides guidance on best practice relating to disapplication of pre-emption rights.
http://www.pre-emptiongroup.org.uk/

The Investor Relations Society

Represents IR practitioners, posts useful guidelines on matter such as website and annual report presentation.
http://www.ir-soc.org.uk

Not-for-profit organisations that promote good governance

Tomorrow's Company

A highly influential UK-based, not-for-profit think-tank that describes itself as: 'a not-for-profit research and agenda setting organisation committed to creating a future for business which makes equal sense to staff, shareholders and society'.
http://www.tomorrowscompany.com/default.aspx

Forceforgood

An online community sponsored by Tomorrow's Company to debate important business issues and to promote business as a force for good.
http://www.forceforgood.com/

Institute of Business Ethics

Charity that encourages high standards of business behaviour based on ethical values, through conferences, publications, research, advocacy and training.
http://www.ibe.org.uk/

International Corporate Governance Network

ICGN members are largely institutional investors who collectively represent funds under management of around US$9.5 trillion. It 'works to raise standards of corporate governance worldwide'.
www.icgn.org

European Corporate Governance Institute

An international not-for-profit association that promotes best practice in corporate governance through commissioning and publishing research and encouraging debate.
http://www.ecgi.org/

The Global Corporate Governance Forum

Part of the World Bank, dedicated to improving corporate governance in emerging markets and developing countries.
www.gcgf.org

Employers' Forum on Disability

An employers' organisation that aims to make it easier for companies to recruit and retain disabled employees and to serve disabled customers.
http://www.employers-forum.co.uk

The London Benchmarking Group (LBG)

Consists of leading international corporations who manage, measure and report their involvement in the community.
http://www.lbg-online.net

Race for Opportunity

A business-led network of private and public sector organisations working on race and diversity through enhancing the competitiveness of its supporters by creating an inclusive management environment and recognition of the economic potential of ethnic minorities.
http://www.raceforopportunity.co.uk

United Nations Environment Programme (UNEP)

Prudential is a signatory to UNEP's Financial Institutions' Statement on the Environment and Sustainable Development and is a member of the Climate Change work group.
http://www.unepfi.net

Advice on board effectiveness

Institute of Directors (IOD)

The IOD gives advice on the duties and responsibilities which being a director entails.

http://www.iod.com/Home/Business-Information-and-advice/Being-a-Director/Duties-and-Responsibilties/

Financial Reporting Council (FRC)

The FRC publishes guidance on issues pertaining to board effectiveness. http://www.frc.org.uk/images/uploaded/documents/Guidance%20on%20board%20effectiveness%20FINAL6.pdf

Department of Trade and Industry (DTI)

The DTI published its report Building Better Boards in 2004. http://www.bis.gov.uk/files/file19615.pdf

Blogs

A number of blog sites provide interesting articles, news of developments and also links to other information sites, so that a browse here may lead to many other resources and ideas.

This blog from Tricker and Mallin, two British professors in the governance field, unashamedly promotes their books, but they also have sensible things to say. http://corporategovernanceoup.wordpress.com/

Blog by Robert Goddard a law and governance lecturer at Aston University. http://corporatelawandgovernance.blogspot.com/

US-based site with around 15 contributors, encouraging discussion on issues, ideas and news on gogernance. http://corporategovernanceforum.blogspot.com/

Another US-based site but with an extensive list of links, many international. http://corpgov.net

There is, of course, my own blog. http://finchesblog.blogspot.com

Watchdogs

The following are some organisations that provide friendly and some not so friendly criticism of governments and companies.

Transparency International

Transparency International is a global civil society organisation working against corruption through research, publicity and advocacy.
http://www.transparency.org/

Corporate Watch

Avowedly anti-corporate campaigning website. It undertakes research on the social and environmental impact of large corporations, particularly multinationals. Its declared aim is to expose the detrimental effects corporations have on society and the environment.
http://www.corporatewatch.org.uk/

Somo – Centre for Research on Multinational Companies

Dutch-based, anti-corporatist website.
http://somo.nl/

Ethical investment

FTSE4Good Index Series

Established in 2001, part of the Financial Times Index service, designed to measure the performance of companies that meet globally recognised corporate responsibility standards, and to facilitate investment in those companies.
http://www.ftse.com/Indices/FTSE4Good_Index_Series/index.jsp

EIRIS

A UK-based, independent, not-for-profit organisation providing research into the environmental, social, governance (ESG) and ethical performance of companies.
http://www.eiris.org/

APCIMS

The Association of Private Client Investment Managers and Stockbrokers is the trade association of 217 wealth management and broking firms.
http://www.apcims.co.uk/

Calpers

The California Public Employees Retirement System is the largest US public pension fund with assets exceeding $210bn. It has a strong ethical and corporate governance stance and is known as an activist investor.
http://www.calpers-governance.org/

Ceres

A US-based network of investors, environmental organisations and other public interest groups working with companies and investors to address sustainability challenges such as global climate change.
http://www.ceres.org

Consultants and advice

There are many areas connected to governance where external consultants may contribute objectivity, experience and the distance that is necessary. Although there are very many consultancy firms, just a few are given as examples of subject areas covered. These are independent firms, although many big audit practices also have consultancy arms that may deal with these issues. I am a little uncertain that using one's own auditor for such advice is, itself, good governance practice.

GovernanceMetrics International

A research and consultancy organisation addressing corporate governance worldwide. It provides governance risk ratings on major corporations worldwide.
http://www.gmiratings.com/

PIRC

the UK's 'leading independent research and advisory consultancy' providing services to institutional investors on corporate governance and corporate social responsibility.
http://www.pirc.co.uk

The Scala Group

HR Consultancy operating in the UK and continental Europe, covering leadership, board effectiveness and Talent Management, coaching, assessment and development.
www.thescalagroup.co.uk

Iddas

Consultancy covering board effectiveness, coaching and assessment.
http://www.iddas.com/

Goodcorporation

A for-profit consultancy advising businesses on codes of conduct, compliance, ethical behaviour and reputation management.
http://www.goodcorporation.com/about-us.php

Manifest

This commercial, proxy voting agency provides research on the governance of companies to clients and provides an execution service for voting. It also runs a blog on governance issues.
http://blog.manifest.co.uk/

Whistleblowing

Public Concern at Work

The whistleblowing charity that offers advice to individuals and organisations as well as informing public policy.
http://www.pcaw.co.uk/

The British Standards Institute

The Institute publishes a detailed code and guidance on whistleblowing arrangements, produced in association with Public Concern at Work.
http://www.bsigroup.com/en/sectorsandservices/Forms/PAS-19982008-Whistleblowing/

Shareholders Rights

Website that advises on minority shareholder rights.
http://www.shareholderrights.co.uk/disputes_nf.htm

Data

Office for National Statistics (ONS)

Share ownership data are available from ONS.
www.statistics.gov.uk/statbase/product.asp?vlnk=930

London Stock Exchange

The London Stock Exchange is a good sources for all types of business-related data.
www.londonstockexchange.com

Government and regulatory sites

Department for Business, Innovation and Skills

www.berr.gov.uk

Financial Reporting Council

www.frc.org.uk

Financial Services Authority

www.fsa.gov.uk

The European Commission: EU documents

http://ec.europa.eu/internal_market/company/

The briberyact.com

This website provides links, articles and information specifically on the UK's Bribery Act 2010.
www.thebriberyact.com

Reports and guidelines

Cadbury Report

http://www.ecgi.org/codes/documents/cadbury.pdf

Greenbury Report

http://www.ecgi.org/codes/documents/greenbury.pdf

Hampel Report

http://www.ecgi.org/codes/documents/hampel.pdf

Higgs Report

http://www.ecgi.org/codes/code.php?code_id=121

Smith Report on audit committees

http://www.fide.org.my/publications/reports/0008_rep_20081211.pdf

Turnbull Report

http://www.ecgi.org/codes/documents/turnbul.pdf

Walker Review

http://www.hm-treasury.gov.uk/d/walker_review_261109.pdf

Financial Reporting Council Guidance

http://www.frc.org.uk/documents/pagemanager/frc/FRC%20The%20UK%20Approach%20to%20Corporate%20Governance%20final.pdf

IOD Four Key Tasks for the board

http://www.iod.com/Home/Training-and-Development/Chartered-Director/Mainwebsite/Resources/Document//training_Chart_Dir_Key_Tasks.pdf

London Stock Exchange – Listing Rules

http://fsahandbook.info/FSA/html/handbook/LR

The King III report and guidelines from the Institute of Directors in South Africa

http://african.ipapercms.dk/IOD/KINGIII/kingiiireport/

Corporate social responsibility

AccountAbility

An international organisation which develops tools and standards for organisational accountability.
www.accountability.org

Sustainability

A think-tank and consultancy advising clients on corporate responsibility and sustainable development.
www.sustainability.com

The Carbon Trust

Not-for-profit company supporting business and the public sector in cutting carbon emissions, saving energy and commercialising low-carbon technologies.
http://www.carbontrust.co.uk/Pages/Default.aspx

ClientEarth

'An organisation of activist lawyers committed to securing a healthy planet... bringing together law, science and policy to create pragmatic solutions to key environmental challenges.'
http://www.clientearth.org/

Forum for the Future

A sustainable development charity working in partnership with business and the public sector. Partner companies include names such as PepsiCo, Vodafone and AkzoNobel.
www.forumforthefuture.org.uk

Global Reporting Initiative

European-based organisation developing a 'sustainability reporting framework'.
http://www.globalreporting.org/

Courses

Many universities and business schools run degree courses on governance and, in addition, they may run executive courses. The Institute of Directors runs short courses for directors as well as longer courses that can lead eventually to chartered director status; The Institute of Company Secretaries and Administrators runs short training courses too.

Books

There are many books related to corporate governance, but most seem to be textbooks aligned to courses; those listed below provide just a small and partial selection of the more impressive ones, aimed at a more general market, that I have come across.

Corporate Governance and Chairmanship, Sir Adrian Cadbury, Oxford University Press, 2002
Cadbury's original code from 1992 is worthwhile but this later book is more readable and contains much wisdom.

Corporate Governance: Principles, Policies and Practices, Bob Tricker, Oxford University Press, 2009
Although this is a textbook from one of the founders of this discipline, it is particularly good and easy to read.

Thin on Top: How to Measure and Improve Board Performance (2nd edn), Bob Garratt, Nicholas Brealey, 2003
Has some strong views but provides a thought-provoking read.

Also
The Fish Rots from the Head: Developing Effective Board Directors (3rd edn), Bob Garratt, Profile Books

The Director's Handbook, Martin Webster, Kogan Page (and the IOD), 2010
Produced by lawyers, this is a legal background for directors.

The Value of Talent, Janice Caplan, Kogan Page, 2010
Addresses talent management from the viewpoint of an integrated and inclusive approach to running organisations, which therefore impinges on governance.

OECD Principles of Corporate Governance, issued in 1999 (revised 2004) in direct response to the Asian financial crisis
An influential and international perspective.

Index